WILLIAM MORROW AND COMPANY, INC.
NEW YORK

For Roger Dowdy

Copyright © 1973 by Andrew Dowdy

Originally published in hardcover by William Morrow and Company, Inc., under the title *"Movies Are Better Than Ever": Wide-Screen Memories of the Fifties.*

First Morrow Paperback Editions printing 1975

Printed in the United States of America.

1 2 3 4 5   79 78 77 76 75

Library of Congress Cataloging in Publication Data

Dowdy, Andrew (date)
  The films of the fifties.

  Published in 1973 under title: "Movies are better than ever."
  Bibliography: p.
  1. Moving-pictures—United States—History.
I. Title.
PN1993.5.U6D6   1975   791.43'0973   75-2132
ISBN 0-688-05198-7 pbk.

Preface

This is a book about movies and moviegoing in the fifties. It's also about Hollywood and the country, that loving couple whose long affair underwent abrasive change in the decade of television, McCarthy, and Brigitte Bardot. The idea of examining the movie culture of the fifties began with the evening I won a bottle of Scotch from my friend Jim Burry for recalling a minor detail of an old film. Not the Scotch but the discussion leading up to it prompted me to think about the peculiar distillation of cultural history bottled in old movies.

I could have lost that fifth many times over. As a buff, I'm far down the line in remembering the exact filmography of Marla English, or what Robert Mitchum said on first meeting Jane Russell in *His Kind of Woman* (1951). What I yield to no one on is my continuing wonder at the universality of movies as touchstones of time and place.

Shortly before his death in 1955, Robert Warshow wrote: "The impulse which leads me to a Humphrey Bogart movie has little in common with the impulse which leads me to the novels of Henry James or the poetry of T. S. Eliot." I've tried to remember this distinction, as well as Warshow's wise advice that our affectionate regard for popular culture is no less interesting than our more profound response to high culture. The recent and rapid elevation of moviegoing into the chief index of hip awareness makes such careful sorting of attitudes increasingly difficult.

Films are both our richest and most engaging source of popular mythology. The current trend in movie criticism often tends to lose sight of this fact. The new critics of cinema frequently charge into a thriller by Samuel Fuller armed with the sort of equipment traditionally deployed to root out the ironic meanings of our more difficult artists. As a conditioned reflex, this tendency is harmless and even a little amusing, an example of the continuing ambiguity of our attraction to popular culture.

In this book I wanted to reconstruct some of the more important and entertaining interrelationships between a puzzling era and a medium rapidly changing under a variety of economic and social pressures. I looked especially at the expendable movies, those pictures that flashed across the country in a matter of weeks, exploiting whatever was current—from the rise of McCarthyism to the death of James Dean. These otherwise ephemeral films were often part of durable cycles that survived rather longer and in more subtle ways than the modest pictures of which they were composed.

When I began this project late in 1971, I had the feeling that I was on a rare anthropological retrieval mission. Only months later "remembering the fifties" boomed from a minor national preoccupation to a major business within the nostalgia industry. I should have guessed as much from my own travels. In seeking to evoke memories of the decade from people, I was amazed that films I thought esoteric beyond belief popped to their minds instantly. In the secret hours of the morning intellectuals who ordinarily shopped no lower than Godard in the contemporary movie market would take me aside to discuss the Mamie Van Doren flicks of the fifties. Soon, it was no surprise for me to hear personal recollections about *The Wild One* (1954) or *Creature from the Black Lagoon* (1954) from people who no longer go to the movies at all.

I grew up in the fifties, and some of the memories of what moviegoing meant to those of us who did are included as part of the record. In preparation for this book I saw within eight months nearly five hundred films and took extensive notes on nearly three hundred, an undertaking I wouldn't care to repeat anytime soon. Most of the movie dialogue quoted was taken either from tapes of the sound tracks or shorthand notes transcribed while watching the films. In a few places—easily recognized by buffs and students—I've attempted to recreate significant dialogue from memory. Popular magazines of the period and such trade publications as *Film Daily* and *Daily Variety* were immensely helpful in recreating the sensibility of the fifties. A selective bibliography is included at the end of the book.

Finally, I would like to say that I'm well aware that in concentrating on the fifties as much as on the films themselves I've slighted many artistically important movies. I was more interested in what was characteristic of the period— however fugitive and ephemeral—than what was clearly important in the larger history of the cinema. In the present cultural atmosphere, I feel certain a formal and comprehensive history of the fifties from a more traditional esthetic perspective is on its way. In fact, if 3-D, hot rods, aliens from space, and Jayne Mansfield don't interest you, it may be that what you are looking for is no more than a few shelves away.

Acknowledgments   Numerous people helped with this project in ways ranging from digging through old files to supplying equal amounts of hot coffee and friendly enthusiasm. Terry Drinkwater, Jim Burry, Leigh Peffer, Richard Block, and Toni Strode provided me with everything from obscure facts to frequent injections of encouragement. Special thanks are due Clifford McCarty, who read the manuscript in draft and gently pointed out my wilder departures from historical accuracy. I'm also indebted to my editor, James Landis, who made helpful corrections without once raising his voice, a true gentleman. The staff of the UCLA Theater Arts Library was always good-natured, even after searching for batches of studio memos which occasionally turned out not to exist.

Photographic materials are through the courtesy of Universal, MGM, 20th Century-Fox, Continental Distributing, Columbia, United Artists, RKO, Futurity Films, Warner Bros–Seven Arts, American International, Allied Artists, and Paramount.

Contents

List of Illustrations

"MOVIES

ARE

WIDE-SCREEN
MEMORIES OF
THE FIFTIES

BETTER

THAN

EVER"

1
Gone
With the
Tube

Hollywood wobbled into the fifties wondering where everybody had gone. During the war, movies were the monopoly entertainment. Gas was rationed. Sports were crippled by the draft, racetracks closed. On the radio there was always the news, and the news wasn't always good. Even "Shoo Shoo Baby" reminded families why fathers, sons, and the boys down the block weren't playing softball in the vacant lot anymore. But the movies offered over forty escape hatches each month. In the neighborhood theaters where programs frequently changed three times a week you could see as many as six different films every seven days. Many did. In 1946 an average weekly audience of ninety million spent nearly 1.7 billion dollars on movie admissions—Hollywood's finest hour, never to be repeated in the history of the industry.

By 1950 motion picture attendance was down more than 25 percent from the postwar peak. Worse, Hollywood's share of the recreation dollar had declined 50 percent. Every measurement of the mass popularity of movies was off for the fourth consecutive year. And television was no longer just around the corner. It was coming through the front door at the rate of over seven million sets a year. Business was bad, the outlook worse. Naturally, everybody wanted to help.

Symposiums were held in which educators berated producers for underestimating the audience, while producers, in turn, complained that exhibitors were only real-estate operators without enough sense to keep the gum off the carpet. Arthur Mayer, himself a discerning exhibitor, said the audience wasn't as hot as intellectuals supposed. He was convinced that imports like *Paisan* (1948) fared better than *The Bicycle Thief* (1949) because while you could play "the adult pictures in the little theaters," only "the adultery ones" made it to the larger movie palaces. Critic Manny Farber went Mayer one better. He called the film audience of the early fifties "the worst in history." Especially worthy of contempt were the self-conscious swells whose "Tiffany-styled esthetics" obscured a defective "sense of the basic characteristics of the medium."

In the interests of science the MGM-financed Motion Picture Research Bureau electrically wired subjects in an effort to translate physiological twitchings and flutterings into practical box-office data. But these biological tea leaves were little improvement on a famous executive's formula for measuring the success of a movie by the amount of time it took for his backside to go numb.

Documentary film maker Alexander Klein feared that "unless we act soon to reform our mass media, they will almost certainly succeed in wholly deforming us." He urged the government to create "a kind of cultural TVA" by going into limited film production designed to accelerate the national improvement of taste. But the institutionalization of the cultural preferences of Harry Truman and Dwight Eisenhower was a concept too staggering in its implications to spark the national imagination. And, anyway, the novels of Max Brand were already well represented on the screen.

As to television, the movies tried various forms of ridicule, the most famous of which was a terse exchange between Marilyn Monroe and George Sanders in *All About Eve* (1950). When Monroe, as a budding delight, inquires if they have auditions for television, Sanders coolly replies, "Auditions, my dear, are *all* they have on television." In *As Young As You Feel* (1951) the upper middle-class living room is conspicuously dominated by an ancient but beautiful radio over which, in a feeble last moment of historical credibility, Junior faithfully listens to swing bands. And in Arch Oboler's *The Twonky* (1953) a television set invaded by an interplanetary spirit attempts to dictate family life, a proposition so obviously bizarre the distributors attempted to pass the film off as science fiction.

On a few points there seemed to be general agreement. The postwar audience was more sophisticated, if somewhat laden with the new responsibility for the most ferocious consumption of goods in the history of Western civilization. Advertising was often offensive. Many agreed with *Commonweal* editor John Cogley that if Hollywood wanted serious consideration by mature filmgoers its lobby posters shouldn't suggest that "the industry is simply a highly organized scheme to merchandise French postcards that talk." The number of art theaters had expanded from around fifty at the close of the war to more than five hundred by 1950. To some this was an index of the growing need for more films intended for adult audiences. But Florence Parry, the drama editor for the Pittsburgh *Press,* worried that a profile of movie interests based on urban culture would neglect the American heartland:

. . . Nothing could work such a hardship upon the population of this country *as a whole* as to withdraw from production and general consumption the motion pictures designed to fit the capacities of the unnumbered millions who, denied the opportunities and benefits vouchsafed the favored minority, are receiving the very kind of entertainment they most enjoy *and need*. . . .

Universal, in the early fifties one of the most family-oriented studios, bailed itself out of the red with the Ma and Pa Kettle series aimed directly at the nabes and small towns Florence Parry was afraid Hollywood would overlook in its cultivation of the city slicker.

At thirteen in 1949 I was no city slicker. But when the Falcon lost his bandage in *Search For Danger* (1949), I knew something was going wrong with the movies. I don't know how old John Calvert was, but after George Sanders and his brother, Tom Conway, he was the last and weakest of the three actors who made the series one of the great trash treasures of the forties. RKO had produced the original Falcon with Edward Dmytryk and Joseph H. Lewis among the more interesting directors sharpening their tools on the Michael Arlen character. In *Search For Danger* the Falcon wore a bandage patch where he "was massaged on the head by a pistol." In one scene Calvert tenderly patted his bandage, while in the next, supposedly occurring minutes later, it was gone. Not thrown away, not blown away, not removed lovingly by Myrna Dell—just gone.

The way I figured it at thirteen there were only two possibilities. They forgot about it. Or they arrogantly assumed the audience was too inattentive to notice anything as trivial as a bandage. Maybe on television in 1949 I wouldn't have noticed such a detail. But the movies were supposed to be different.

Of course they weren't. Any fan of the late lates is familiar with countless similar goofs in the tackier pictures of the forties. Director-producer George Sidney told a UCLA film class that the technical deficiencies of older movies were "as obvious as a barn door." In fact, the industry should be ashamed "if its pictures of ten years ago didn't look old and tired" as they showed up on television. Before 1950, when fewer than one home in eight had a television receiver, movies could still puff along with missing bandages, monster costumes handed down from the previous year, and sets that looked as if they were made out of the same plywood as the the scripts.

In 1950 seven and a half million sets were sold, up from only sixty-five hundred in 1946 and less than a million in 1948. The figure was exceeded only once again in the decade. By 1960 *Television Magazine* estimated 87 percent of all homes had receivers, with penetration well over 90 percent in major American cities. In the intervening years the movies competed against not only inferior examples of their own previous history but also against the family-oriented shows developed specifically for the television audience. The passive habit customers for inoffensive repetitious program pictures had found a new theater in their own living rooms. The screen was smaller, but the popcorn was cheaper and the old man could ease the day's tensions on beer instead of expensive soft drinks with too much ice.

Early fifties research into changing behavior patterns of television viewers led to the hysterical fear that nobody over thirty was ever going to the movies again. A *New York Times* analysis of one hundred areas heavily penetrated by television found motion picture attendance down between 20 and 40 percent. The Charles Alldredge survey of four hundred TV families indicated a decline in monthly moviegoing of 72 percent for adults and 46 percent for children. The 33 percent decline in time devoted to reading was no compensation. A study of Stamford, Connecticut, high school students revealed they averaged twenty-seven hours in front of the tube each week, only one hour less than they spent in school. Much of this time was logged watching old movies. Instead of browsing through the library, students were browsing through old films. In 1956 a Sindlinger and Company survey placed the daily average of TV viewers at seventy-one million, with more than a third of these watching movies for an estimated ten and a half hours each week. In other words, about twenty-five million people were seeing between seven and nine pictures a week free. As economist Michael Conant generously put it, "If these surveys are accurate, it is surprising that movie attendance dropped only 25 percent from 1950 to 1956."

Exhibitors were hit hardest. Writer Don Mankiewicz said they should show the pictures in the street, thereby driving the people into the movie houses. The owners of the nearly three thousand hardtop theaters which closed between 1950 and 1953 weren't very amused. A Chicago confection outfit offered fruit-flavored popcorn in a frank exploitation of the fact that profitable revenue frequently depended more on snack sales than ticket admissions. In California a beleaguered exhibitor gave way entirely, installing television sets inside his theater and rearranging the seats around them. It was illegal to charge admission and so he hoped to make it on the sale of refreshments alone. But people preferred watching Uncle Miltie in drag in the privacy of their own homes.

At a meeting of the Theater Owners of America a speaker unaccustomed to thinking on his feet tried to articulate his frustration. "The movie business is getting too complicated," he complained. "What with having to look at six pictures in order to buy one and keeping the popcorn machine in working order, I just can't find time to sit home with my family and watch television." He brought the house down, but the laughter was a little ragged around the edges. By the mid-fifties the Council of Motion Picture Organizations announced that more than half the nation's nineteen thousand theaters were barely breaking even. Over five thousand were operating at a loss, likely candidates to become meeting halls for men's organizations, or, in larger cities, parking lots between more successful enterprises.

The "CinemaScope rebound," described in a later chapter, was fading by late 1955. Many insiders had darkly predicted that technological novelties were like adrenalin poured into a patient dying of more serious maladies than small screens with flat images in black-and-white. An important producer at Fox, the first studio to commit itself exclusively to the wide screen, gave "the new era just twenty-four months." By 1957 theater admissions were off 26 percent from a year earlier, a decline all the more serious because it nullified the moderate gains in each of the previous three years. In fact, 1957 was the worst year for the movies in the last fifteen. But 1958 would be worse yet, with the box-office gross dropping below the billion-dollar mark for the first time since before the war. Another decade would pass before a billion-dollar annual gross would be equaled again.

In late 1952 producer Jerry Wald told a class in the USC cinema department that "today's movie audiences are discriminating people, while television viewers, for the most part, are not." It had the sound of an official myth, a declaration of respect for moviegoers ironically tendered as they disappeared from their accustomed place on line in front of the box office. Television, in the new mythology, would rot the brain, reducing families to collective zombie tribes unable to read, converse, or eat food unless it was frozen into metal trays and covered with aluminum foil. On certain days during the runs of quiz shows like "Twenty-One" and "The $64,000 Question," theater owners prayed for hot contestants like Herb Stempel or Charles Van Doren to get knocked out of their glass booths the way farmers prayed for rain.

As early as 1949 *Fortune* sensed the end of an era when a staff-written article suggested that "the time may have come" for at least the beginning of an adjustment to the fragmenting mass audience for film. The magazine called for a concept of pluralism which included more ambitious variety than the simple reshuffling of genre programmers. The same year a writer whose income had depended heavily on the durability of oaters and weepies found his services terminated as the studios cut back long-term contracts. He sold his house in the hills and as he departed Hollywood for a newspaper job in the East lamented the passing of the old easy days. "The swimming pools are drying up all over Hollywood," he told Budd Schulberg. "I do not think I shall see them refilled in my generation."

The first and most serious casualty of the television invasion was the B film, especially the low-budget-series picture whose bland familiarity was the essence of the new television programming. When Monogram disappeared in 1953 into its own subsidiary, Allied Artists, more than a change in name was involved. It symbolized the end of a kind of picture for which Monogram and Republic were famous in the forties. Despite Trucolor and Vera Hruba Ralston, Republic headed for the last roundup in 1958. With the extinction of the two the Saturday afternoon Western vanished. Memories of Sunset Carson, Whip Wilson, Johnny Mack Brown, and countless others lingered in odd hours of the television day. Old cowboys were sustained by a new generation of car salesmen who kicked tires and pounded hoods obnoxious decibels above the gentle clopping of horses after bad men or the twanging guitar of Tito Guizar.

In 1950 the Hopalong Cassidy craze caused columnist Sidney Skolsky to blast Hollywood for not properly exploiting the old Hoppy films for "the public eager to see him." The invidious impact of free television movies apparently was difficult to accept—even for professionals. Not enough Hoppy fans anted up to keep Melody Ranch open, and Gene Autry and Roy Rogers both rode off for the safer reaches of network stables. The original Trigger was stuffed so at least something of the old Western tradition was preserved for future pilgrims who found their way to Rogers' museum in Apple Valley, California.

The great detectives—Dick Tracy, Michael Shane, the Falcon, and Charlie Chan—never even made it out of the forties. No replacements appeared in the fifties, the only decade in the history of sound films that failed to produce a recurrent detective hero; unless we include Mickey Spillane's Mike Hammer, who was never played twice by the same actor, a condition so injurious to the continuity of image that Spillane was finally driven into playing the role himself in *The Girl Hunters* (1963). Natural companions of the Western and detective movies were the serials which Republic and Columbia surprisingly kept alive through the middle of the decade. After more than five hundred serials dating back to the early days of silent film, the form expired in 1956 as Lee Roberts went *Blazing the Overland Trail* one last time for Columbia.

By 1959 only indestructible Tarzan remained, lone rem-

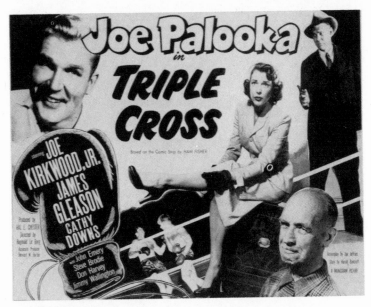

MONOGRAM
Triple Cross: Waning audiences ko'd Joe Palooka, as well as most of the other innocent family programmers inherited from the forties.

Francis in the Haunted House: Mickey Rooney lights the way to television for Francis, the Talking Mule, in the final picture in the popular series.

nant of the series picture, a dominant form of family entertainment for moviegoers of the forties. The rest were gone, every last one. Some slipped away quietly like Maggie and Jiggs and Joe Palooka. Others, like Blondie or Boston Blackie, found new homes, at least temporarily, on television. Francis, the talking mule, was transmogrified into Ed, the talking horse. A few drifted on against the relentless trend away from the innocent era when parents and children were catered to on the same double bill. Mickey Rooney returned to Carvel one last time in *Andy Hardy Comes Home* (1958). But both Lewis Stone and Louis B. Mayer were dead, and dreamy clips of Judy Garland and Lana Turner from earlier films only emphasized the historical past the movies had left behind. The Bowery Boys, descendants through the East Side Kids from the dock gang in Sidney Kingsley's 1935 Broadway play *Dead End*, were the most pathetic extension of the series concept. Well into their late thirties, Leo Gorcey and Huntz Hall, as Muggs and Glimpy, hopelessly perpetuated the image of a gang of boys in which none of the members had been a *boy* for the better part of two decades.

Comedy teams, another staple of family film entertainment, also disappeared in the fifties. The Marx Brothers made *Love Happy* (1950) their last film together, while Groucho lingered on in *Double Dynamite* (1951) and *A Girl in Every Port* (1952), neither of which deserved him. Abbott & Costello routinely met everything on the Universal-International lot from the Mummy and Frankenstein to Martians composed of U-I's contract starlets, but like many other comedians they were competing against their own television programs. *Dance With Me, Henry* (1956) was a bland finale, the final shot with Lou as Pied Piper to a long line of skipping children— a touching memento of the career of the chubby clown who, next to Bob Hope, was the most popular comic talent in films of the forties.

In 1948, with Abbott & Costello near the peak of their popularity, Ed Sullivan's first "Toast of the Town" television show introduced nationally a new and even zanier team, Dean Martin and Jerry Lewis. In typical Sullivan fashion they were sandwiched between a boxing referee and a singing fireman. From the next year's appearance as second bananas to Marie Wilson in *My Friend Irma* (1949) they quickly soared to box-office success with *At War with the Army* (1951) and fourteen other films concluding with *Hollywood or Bust* (1956). Fan magazines and gossip columns whispered of discontents between the two as early as *Pardners* (1956). When Martin was announced for a solo part in *Ten Thousand Bedrooms* (1957) and Lewis began *The Delicate Delinquent* (1957), with Darren McGavin in the role expectation would have given to Dean, no more needed to be said. At a dinner for Hollywood writers a humorous sketch turned on the auction of the early love letters of Martin & Lewis.

Into the vacuum created by the split between Martin & Lewis and the eclipse of Abbott & Costello plunged other night club acts. Tommy Noonan and Peter Marshall were doomed by the inept pacing of *The Rookie* (1960), but the presence of Julie Newmar in various stages of undress indicated the transition from family fun to nudie cuties Noonan was to make in the sixties. More amusing was *Once Upon a Horse* (1958), a send-up of Westerns with Rowan & Martin in the long days before their shtick was electronically rejuvenated by "Laugh-In." Of all the comedy teams which had come and gone since the early days of sound, only The Three Stooges, with various changes in personnel, continued into the sixties. They were one of the last direct connections in films between the conventions of old-time burlesque and an audience born too late to have seen a man remove live birds, salamis, and a goldfish bowl from his baggy pants anywhere but at the movies.

The saddest example of a tradition wearing itself out in public was in a crass rip-off of Martin & Lewis called *Bela Lugosi Meets a Brooklyn Gorilla* (1953). Sammy Petrillo, an uncanny ringer for Lewis, and his partner, Duke Mitchell, are on their way to entertain the troops when they crash in the jungle, falling into the hands of a Lugosi so tired and afflicted he actually sounds like Lenny Bruce's imitation of him. "Aren't you the one who bites children in the neck?" Petrillo twits him. And for a dazed moment, in his secret jungle laboratory, test tubes mysteriously frothing away, Lugosi looks as if he's not sure. It was all so long ago. Three years later Lugosi was dead, his last films preposterously dated.

More significant than the predictable shift to television of series entertainment was the simultaneous diminution of the harmonious American family as a central image in the films of the fifties. I'm not thinking of the Dagwood syndrome, those befuddled fathers like William Bendix's Riley or Arthur Lake's Bumstead who gravitated from radio or film, or both, to the natural habitat of the small screen. Or the teen-agers, like Henry Aldrich or Corliss Archer, whose continuing predicaments weren't troubling enough to cause knitting mothers to drop a stitch from week to week. Or even the resilient Ozzie & Harriet, who paused only once in *Here Come the Nelsons* (1952) in their smooth transition from radio to television. The gentle rituals of situation comedy were really better suited to the indifferent attention produced by the goings and comings of living room society. Some people read while watching television. Others ate dinner, paid bills, or wrote letters to relatives to whom they devoted only as much interest as could conveniently be shared with the Ricardos on

MGM
Father of the Bride: Spencer Tracy and Joan Bennett in sleepless anxiety over cost of Elizabeth Taylor's wedding. Parents in later fifties films are kept awake by less cheerful rituals—like the chicken race death in *Rebel Without a Cause.*

"I Love Lucy." Radio, after all, was only reclaiming its own, a previous decade's defection to the movies.

The passing of films like *Father of the Bride* (1950) and *Elopement* (1951) involved more than the simple displacement of program entertainment from one medium to another. A complex of values and the celebration of them which had remained intact throughout such forties pictures as *The Human Comedy* (1943), *Since You Went Away* (1944), or *Meet Me in St. Louis* (1944) were no longer sustainable. At least not with the confident sense of tradition which flourished at its durable best during the war.

Samuel Goldwyn's *I Want You* (1951) displayed unsightly twitches in the American family's reflexive patriotism. Robert Keith, who obscenely romanticizes combat with a living room full of war trophies won exclusively in Sixth Avenue pawn shops, sends his younger son, Farley Granger, off to Korea with the sodden toast, "to kill a lot of them." The reluctant son explodes. "Why not drop the bomb if that's what the old men want?" The movie views neither attitude sympathetically. But the ambiguities of the Cold War as its political consequences heated up in Korea had no parallel in the simpler world where Robert Hutton dated Joan Leslie at the *Hollywood Canteen* (1944) and John Hodiak tipped the wings of his plane in a farewell salute to Anne Baxter, Gramps, and the kids in *Sunday Dinner for a Soldier* (1944).

Father of the Bride and its sequel, *Father's Little Dividend* (1951), were among the last films of any excellence to convey in detail as rich as it was credible family life in which the generations were congruent, their hopes and ambitions uncritically defined by the middle American ethic. Vincente Minnelli was a fine MGM exponent of this sentiment, particularly as it turned on the desire toward upward mobility and the domestic conflicts created by the genteel anxieties of the upward bound. Spencer Tracy and Joan Bennett were the sort of superparents Elizabeth Taylor required, while Don

Taylor repeated the popular role of the American boy-man played by Tom Drake in Minnelli's *Meet Me in St. Louis.*

Then came Brando's cycle gang, James Dean, Vic Morrow cutting up Teach, and American-International's violent youth-culture flicks. After the mid-fifties the naïveté and wonder of Elizabeth and Don coming of age amidst Daddy's war with officious caterers was out of sync. *House Beautiful* ideas of outdoor weddings were too effete for a screen full of tough kids out of families with problems more serious than surviving the vicissitudes of socially proper conduct. Peter Bogdanovich scored the fact ironically in *The Last Picture Show* (1971) by having Jeff Bridges and Timothy Bottoms watch *Father of the Bride* as one of the last movies to play Ben Johnson's theater in a withering Texas town at the turn of the decade.

Television, in siphoning off the most passive element in the old film audience, actually did the movies a favor. Film makers were forced to cultivate segments in the mass audience whose tastes were not satisfied by tepid and repetitious television fare. These included the sophisticated "lost audience" which historically had identified its cultural interests with the novel and the theater; young people with unprecedented economic power and the more traditional burning inclination to get the hell out of the house; and, of course, the bored millions who needed diversion in which the current was continually hiked through promises and exhortations that at last, just now, they could see what they had never seen before.

In early 1950 the industry, following a lead appearing in advertisements for Loew's theaters in New York and Chicago, adopted a new slogan. It declared at every opportunity, including lettering on the sides of popcorn boxes, that "Movies Are Better Than Ever!" The remainder of this book is the informal record of how this promise fared in what is widely regarded as the most turbulent decade in the history of film.

2

I Married a Communist & Other Disasters of the Blacklist

On February 9, 1950, Senator Joseph McCarthy announced in Wheeling, West Virginia, that he held in his hand a list of two hundred and fifty-seven Communists presently employed in the State Department. Within a month Elizabeth Taylor had married one in MGM's March release, *Conspirator*. America's · most glamorous teen-ager would be better matched later in the summer when she had wise if irascible Spencer Tracy to guide her marriage in *Father of the Bride*. But as of March she symbolized the very seduction of American innocence which increasingly would become McCarthy's message to the country.

It was Junior Miss vs. Marx with Sally Benson's script missing no opportunity to inform us of the mindless totalitarian threat lurking even at fashionable dances in London society. Robert Taylor, as the Communist disguised as a British officer of unusually cool reserve, swept young Elizabeth off her feet. The reserve, we come to suspect, is induced by a party discipline which teaches that notions of a right to private life are ridiculous. Certainly Taylor's effort to explain his political attitude to his wife is. It consists of some opaque remarks about the death of the aristocracy. Elizabeth doesn't get the point.

Still and all, she notices some peculiar things about Taylor. He is indifferent to an injured rabbit in a trap. "After all, it's only a rabbit," he tells her. The discovery of a letter requesting a meeting with a party superior finally brings into focus her husband's insidious social views and his unpatriotic attitude toward rabbits. It all connects and she no longer loves him. The party suggests Elizabeth be eliminated. "You're a soldier, major. You know there are always casualties in war." But in the end the major fluffs even this assignment. The only remaining one is to put on his military uniform and commit suicide.

The portrait of Communists and communism in *Conspirator* was part of Hollywood's effort to atone for the sins disclosed before the House Committee on Un-American Activities in its Hollywood hearings of 1947. According to Chairman J. Parnell Thomas, the Committee was investigating evidence of Communist propaganda in films. Robert Taylor was among those who agreed that Communist activity in the industry had increased after Pearl Harbor. "Life is a little too short to be around people who annoy me as much as these fellow travelers and Communists do," he told the Committee. But offhand he couldn't remember any films specifically Red in nature.

Neither could most of the other friendly witnesses. Adolphe Menjou thought Communist actors might be able to introduce subversive content into film with a mere glance or inflection of the voice, but he couldn't think of a single example at the moment. Still, it was possible. He quit the stand to applause after concluding that "America should arm to the teeth." Ginger Rogers' mother, Mrs. Leila Rogers, whom Representative John McDowell identified as "one of the outstanding experts on communism in the United States," was more specific. She directed her daughter not to appear in a film version of Theodore Dreiser's *Sister Carrie* because of its obvious propaganda content. And she detected, somewhat equivocally, Communist philosophy in Clifford Odets' *None but the Lonely Heart* (1944), especially in a scene where she interpreted Cary Grant's remark to his mother about squeezing "pennies from people poorer than we are" as a nasty jab at free enterprise.

As the hearings developed that October of 1947, little testimony about specific films occupied the Committee. *The North Star* (1943) and *Song of Russia* (1944) were mentioned as examples of films presumably corrupted by the hands of ex-Communists. And *Mission to Moscow* (1943) was forced on Jack Warner by no less a radical than F.D.R. himself. But there was no mention of such frothy tracts as Columbia's *The Boy from Stalingrad* (1943) or PRC's *Miss V from Moscow* (1942), possibly because nobody connected with them had been identified to the Committee as a former or present Communist. It was revisionist history, of course, as if since Churchill's famous Iron Curtain speech in 1946 nobody, except on penalty of public vituperation, could admit that only a few years ago Russia had been our ally. "We have to keep Stalin fighting—and your picture can make a case for him with the American people," Roosevelt told Jack Warner. Warner made *Mission to Moscow*. Westbrook Pegler detected a Red taint, but he was years ahead of his time.

Although Thomas and an aide were photographed examining reels of film frame by frame, even this extraordinary attention to detail uncovered no serious charge of widespread Communist content in American films. In fact, there wasn't any. Or so little that researcher Dorothy B. Jones in her "careful combing of the product" for Red propaganda thought even doubtful instances "so rare that . . . they are extremely difficult to find." Early along it was clear that the unstated intention of the HUAC 1947 hearings was to expose political activities and associations of individuals the

Committee believed either to be party members, Communist sympathizers, or willing dupes of the Communist conspiracy.

Originally, nineteen of those subpoenaed to appear in Washington by HUAC decided in some measure to be unfriendly witnesses. Their personal reasons included variously the belief that the Committee had no right to inquire into private political affiliations and the fear that public exposure of unpopular political attitudes would lead to economic hardship or worse in the Cold War pathology of the late forties. Ring Lardner Jr.'s response to the fourth request that he answer whether or not he was a member of the Communist party probably expressed the attitude with which most unfriendly witnesses were in accord. "I could answer it [i.e., the question]," he told Chairman Thomas, "but if I did I would hate myself in the morning."

After ten of the unfriendly nineteen were called, the hearings abruptly terminated with subsequent citations of contempt for each of those who had appeared. The Hollywood Ten was born and the institutionalization of the notorious blacklist was under way.* Developing industry protest over the treatment of the Hollywood Ten was quickly intimidated by a meeting of the executive and financial leaders of the film community at the Waldorf-Astoria in New York in November of 1947. The Waldorf Statement, as it came to be known, censured the actions of the Ten and spelled out official industry policy. Those among the Ten currently employed would be summarily fired. They would not be re-employed until they were either "acquitted" or "purged" of the contempt charges and declared themselves under oath not to be Communists. Further, the studios would "not

---

* One more time for the record, the original Ten who were indicted for contempt were: Alvah Bessie, Herbert Biberman, Lester Cole, Edward Dmytryk, Ring Lardner Jr., John Howard Lawson, Albert Maltz, Samuel Ornitz, Adrian Scott, and Dalton Trumbo.

knowingly employ a Communist or a member of any party
or group which advocates the overthrow of the Government
of the United States by force or by any illegal or unconstitutional methods." The Waldorf Statement admitted the risk
of "creating an atmosphere of fear" and concluded with a
salute to the patriotic "30,000 Americans employed in
Hollywood who have given our Government invaluable aid
in war and peace." A few days later Ed Sullivan tersely explained the less public implications of the New York meeting. Wall Street investment in movie companies was in the
neighborhood of sixty million. "Wall Street jiggled the strings,
thas all."

By the early fifties the Ten were in jail, their last judicial
appeal exhausted when the Supreme Court refused review of
their case. Alger Hiss was also in jail, a vastly symbolic
figure in whom many Americans saw a malignant relationship between the New Deal and the Communist Left. Journalist Alistair Cooke called the long confrontation between
Hiss and Whittaker Chambers the drama of a "generation
on trial." The Halloween image of Chambers leading HUAC
member Richard Nixon into a patch of hollowed pumpkins in
which was hidden microfilm of stolen State Department
documents was as prophetic as it was bizarre. The witch-
hunts of the fifties produced no scenario more dramatic or
controversial than the Hiss case. For critic Leslie Fiedler
it marked the end of an era. Finding a demonic evil in
Hiss's refusal to confess his guilt, Fiedler wrote that for
American liberalism "the age of innocence is dead." In the
guise of topicality, Fox's *The Big Lift* (1950) perfectly illustrated the adjustments in the innocent trustfulness of the
American character required by the Cold War.

Paul Douglas and Montgomery Clift are two NCO's
transferred from Hawaii to Germany during the Berlin
blockade. Douglas is brash and sadistic. His German girl
friend "gives me one-day service on my laundry. The PX

takes a week." To the more naïve and trusting Clift he gives uncluttered romantic advice. "Swing at the first pitch." But cheap kraut ass isn't what the moody and idealistic Clift is after. He wants to marry his girl, even after finding she has deceived him about the real sympathy her relatives had for Hitler. Douglas isn't surprised about either the German or Russian character. "I've yet to meet a German that wasn't drafted," he sneers. On his arrival in Berlin he says to another soldier, "This is where they should have dropped the A-Bomb."

Both Douglas and Clift are ambassadors of the American style of mind in the postwar years. Douglas, awkward and bombastic, endlessly fumbles to explain the nature of a democratic society to his unbelieving German mistress. Truman was elected "despite newspapers and bookies." But when was the last time a "Ruskie saw anything but Stalin on a ballot?" Clift is forgiving, generous—a Lon McCallister type longing to be back home in Indiana but making

20TH CENTURY-FOX
The Big Lift: Montgomery Clift and Paul Douglas as contrasting representatives of the American style of mind in George Seaton's interesting study of innocence and experience in post-war Europe.

the best of the incomprehensible ironies of the Cold War world. "What do you want to do, start another war?" he asks when Douglas abuses a German DP.

Our sympathies are clearly directed to Clift, which only makes the denouement darker in its implications. He has badly misjudged the long-term damage done by the war. His girl turns out to be part of an immoral generation brought up on lies. She was only using Clift to get to the States to see a boyfriend in St. Louis. The discovery is disillusioning. He was too open, too innocent. For balance, Douglas is consoling, more humanized. He could be a "better salesman" for America if he was less the "storm trooper." But he has the unstated satisfaction of proving the better historian, the more astute representative of the unsentimental toughness required of America in dealing with a morally corrupt Europe.

In the 1947 HUAC hearings, Chairman Thomas asked director and friendly witness Leo McCarey if he thought the industry should produce anti-Communist films to educate the public about the dangers of the Communist party in the United States. McCarey stumbled through an answer which seemed to suggest that Donald Duck was about the apex of screen achievement and a more acceptable goal for Hollywood than propaganda. The message, for the moment, may have missed McCarey, but to the rest of the industry it was loud and clear. Between the summer of 1948 and HUAC's second set of Hollywood hearings beginning in March of 1951, the studios released no less than a dozen anti-Communist pictures. While a little tardy, Leo McCarey made his own contribution in 1952 with *My Son John*, one of the most odious in a cycle noted for its frequent lunatic pitch.

In the 1952 Presidential campaign, Eisenhower's running mate, Richard Nixon, attacked Adlai Stevenson for a deposition of good character he had written for Hiss during the latter's trials for perjury. The implication was that Stevenson's political judgment was insidiously dangerous to the country. By these standards the capacity of mere movie folk to wreak havoc on the nation was incalculable. Not just Communists and ex-Communists—but anyone who had joined or loaned his name to a group judged retroactively un-American had to confess his guilt and name his associates or be driven from the industry.

To aid the studios a variety of private and patriotic organizations gratuitously provided producers with information useful in determining the employability of talent. The Motion Picture Alliance for the Preservation of American Ideals— a group of political conservatives including Rupert Hughes, Ward Bond, Ayn Rand, and others—aided actors in "purging" themselves of past political blunders. The American Legion was also eager to assist. A December, 1951, article in its national magazine asked coyly, "Did the Movies Really Clean House?" The Legion's answer was a loud NO and it had lists of currently employed persons with Red associations in their pasts to prove its case. Founded by three former FBI agents in 1947, *Counterattack* and its sister publication *Red Channels* were committed to driving "people with continuing records of pro-Communist activity" from all aspects of show business.

But by far the most vicious and inflammatory of the self-appointed guardians of the American Way was Myron C. Fagan. Through his Cinema Educational Guild, he issued subliterate pamphlets such as *Documentation of the Red Stars in Hollywood* and *Red Treason in Hollywood*. An advertisement for the latter claimed that it named between two and three hundred movie personalities "who enabled Moscow to get control of our Screen." What constituted such control was indicated by one of Fagan's printed lectures from 1950. Under the heading "Hollywood Reds Still At It!" he attacked Fox's important if bleak indictment of racism, *No Way Out* (1950). He described "Darryl Zanuch [sic]" as "that pro-

ducer who was responsible for *Gentleman's Agreement*
[1947], *Pinky* [1949], and other Films which so effectively
advance Red ideology." To the charge that his direct attacks
had resulted in the smearing or blacklisting of Eddie Cantor,
Danny Kaye, and Paul Muni, Fagan replied, "I take it as
eulogy."

The "atmosphere of fear" warned against in the Waldorf
Statement had become a reality. The rooting out of present
members of the Communist party had degenerated into an
attack on anyone who, past or present, engaged in controversial political or social activity. Major studios maintained
"clearance men," whose job was to certify a clean bill of political health for all current or potential employees. But accumulated accusations could come from sources as various as
HUAC testimony, Fagan-type self-patriots, or even the whispered innuendo of vindictive gossips.

After the 1951–52 HUAC Hollywood hearings, the blacklist expanded rapidly with the proliferating number of
individuals identified as former Communists by friendly witnesses. It was the chain-letter effect. Those previously blacklisted could clear themselves by cooperative testimony citing
still other ex-Commmnists who were themselves candidates
for the list unless they confessed and contributed their own
additions.

The blacklist closed in on people sometimes directly, sometimes in oblique and coded ways. Joseph Losey remembered
turning down an RKO project *I Married a Communist*
(1949): "I later learned this was a touchstone for establish-
ing who was not 'a red': you offered *I Married a Communist*
to anybody you thought was a Communist, and if they turned
it down, they were." Twelve others followed Losey in refusing the film before Robert Stevenson directed it with Robert
Ryan as the ex-Commie unable to break free of the party in
the form of oily Thomas Gomez. By 1951 Losey was blacklisted. Abraham Polonsky pleaded the Fifth Amendment be-

fore HUAC in 1951. He received no directorial credits between *Force of Evil* in 1949 and *Tell Them Willie Boy Is Here* twenty years later. Asked by film critic William Pechter how he knew he was blacklisted, he replied, "I was told by the studio, my agent, newspapers, Congress, and my landlord." Screenwriter Donald Ogden Stewart joked about the fate of radicals in Hollywood in an ironic speech before the League of American Writers in 1937. But after he wrote the screenplay for *Edward, My Son* (1949) MGM summoned him for a more serious discussion of the subject. He preferred silence and exile in England to the answers he knew were required.

Stewart was one of one hundred and sixty-one individuals identified as Communists by screenwriter Martin Berkeley in an extended confession which easily broke the House Committee record for friendly information. Other names on Berkeley's list included: Sidney Buchman, Howard da Silva, Guy Endore, Carl Foreman, Dorothy Parker, Robert Rossen, Waldo Salt, and Budd Schulberg. Schulberg had already confessed. Rossen had previously denied party membership. But the blacklist changed his mind, and he admitted Communist affiliation in May of 1953. Even so he had no directorial credits between 1951 and *Mambo* in 1955. Buchman was cited for contempt but got off cheap with a $150 fine and a suspended sentence. Still, he was blacklisted, along with most of the others on Berkeley's prodigious list. Subsequent to his testimony, Berkeley joined the Motion Picture Alliance, where he was celebrated as its chief authority on communism in the industry.

The conflict of conscience posed by an HUAC subpoena engendered enormous personal bitterness. Some witnesses informed with fervor like Martin Berkeley, who believed that anyone who "joined the party since 1945 and who retains his membership today is a traitor." At the opposite pole were those, like the Hollywood Ten, who in no way would cooperate with the hearings, regarding them as unconstitutional witch-hunts. Others took Lillian Hellman's position that they would openly discuss their own political past but would not identify associates who could be innocently hurt. But the Committee denied this option because it could not "permit witnesses to set forth the terms under which they will testify." And, finally, among friendly witnesses were those like Elia Kazan, who, weighing the dangers of contemporary communism against a moral reluctance to inform, decided in favor of cooperative testimony.

No doubt few positions were pure of the economic fear of the blacklist. And nobody could tell which way the chips would fall. Larry Parks pleaded for the Committee not to force him to name others before capitulating to its demands in executive testimony. But Columbia suspended him on receipt of his subpoena and his career never recovered the momentum of his popular Jolson movies. Kazan publicly stated that following his HUAC appearance Fox cut his salary in half, explaining that he was now "a controversial character." And many years later screenwriter Borden Chase blamed his inactivity in the sixties on his prominent anti-Communist work for the Motion Picture Alliance in the fifties. "Now they're in the saddle," he explained, "and they make it very, very hard."

Going to the movies in the election year of 1952 you were lucky if you didn't see at least several specimens from Hollywood's most vigorous crop of anti-Communist pictures. Twelve were produced that year. It was a difficult time to avoid the subject of communism. Jack Anderson wrote a book defining the life and work of the Senator from Wisconsin, whose name in two brief years already signified an era. Columnist George Sokolsky saw no threatening portent in McCarthy's work. The issue was simple. Every candidate, he wrote, "will have to say whether he favors or opposes the employment of Communists in public positions. That is all McCarthyism means." And the historical treachery of Communists in public position was recorded in highly charged prose in the year's most sensational best seller—*Witness* by Whittaker Chambers.

The Presidential campaign of 1952 introduced a new term —*egghead*—to refer to the followers of Adlai Stevenson. A few years later, when asked by a reporter for an interpretation of the expression, Stevenson replied that an egghead was "one who called Marilyn Monroe Mrs. Arthur Miller." That was a more generous definition than many middle Americans supplied in 1952. Novelist Louis Bromfield struck a native chord when he filed his portrait of the egghead "as a person of spurious intellectual pretensions . . . a self-conscious prig, so given to examining all sides of a question that he becomes thoroughly addled while remaining always in the same spot." Moreover, as a *Freeman* editorial put it, eggheads resented Joe McCarthy because he was "constitutionally incapable of deference to social status," especially as reflected in the Eastern establishment of Ivy League button-downs. *Time*, itself a recent object of McCarthy's lack of deference, concluded that the nation's intellectuals were badly out of touch with heartland America. It was a lesson you could learn every day in the anti-Communist movies of the period.

John Agar, Shirley Temple's first husband and an actor whose chief virtue was to play every role as if he were a permanent prisoner aboard the Good Ship Lollipop, was seduced, body and soul, by Communist intellectuals in *I Married a Communist*. You could tell that Janis Carter, as the chief seducer, was an intellectual because she slept with men to whom she was not married, a vice obviously picked up from her membership in the Young Communist League in the thirties. Other intellectuals in the film were readily identifiable because they either looked Jewish or smoked cigarettes held between the index and third fingers, or both.

Agar was as befuddled in his confrontation with Red propaganda as Elizabeth Taylor had been when exposed to Robert Taylor's critique of social classes in *Conspirator*. "Ideologically uninformed but emotionally responsive," we overhear an obnoxious creep report as Agar wanders off complaining to Carter that he should stick to his own league "because they got me all confused." Bumped off follows confused, as William Talman, a bebop killer in a Brew Moore jacket, runs Agar down in the streets, a gangster image of Communist activity repeated throughout the earlier fifties.

Intellectuals were villains again in Leo McCarey's *My Son John*. Robert Walker, in his last role, completed a transformation begun when the young soldier who loved Jennifer Jones in *Since You Went Away* emerged as the postwar psychopath Farley Granger met in *Strangers on a Train* (1951). As a Communist spy, Walker projected beneath a curiously malevolent surface that residual innocence that was his trademark in the forties. The image of something fine corrupted into a cold supercilious sneer was the movie's one powerful quality. The rest was berserk Americana.

Walker's father, Dean Jagger, was a grotesque caricature of the kind of American who thinks all eggheads should love it or leave it, an idea memorialized in his favorite ditty which runs, "If you don't like your Uncle Sammy/Then go back to your home o'er the sea." An apogee of mindless goodness, Jagger is simultaneously an educator, a Catholic, and a member of the American Legion. His outrage with his son reaches a high point when he clouts Walker with a Bible. Ultimately the comrades gun Walker down with the same casualness with which they eliminated Agar in *I Married a Communist*. The mother, Helen Hayes, is given the healing message of the film: think with your heart, not your head. To question home, church, or tradition is the beginning of moral corruption. Many Americans would vote from the cozy restrictions of that perspective later in the year.

The anti-Communist films made conspicuous use of actors like Robert Walker, John Agar, and Elizabeth Taylor in whom audiences could easily identify a sense of endangered or squandered innocence. As an escaped Russian ballet dancer, Janet Leigh spent much of *The Red Danube* (1949) disguised as a nun, before preferring a suicidal leap from a window to forced repatriation in Russia. In Monogram's *The Steel Fist* (1952) former child actor Roddy McDowall portrayed an American student trapped in an Iron Curtain country. There were even Communists among the unsuspecting Eskimos in *Red Snow* (1952). John Wayne abandoned the saddle long enough to track down Reds in Hawaii in *Big Jim McLain* (1952), and Sabu routed Commies from a mythical island with the aid of Sid Melton's monkey in *Savage Drums* (1951). In many of these films the Communist threat was seen from a viewpoint historically rural or small town. It was as if Carvel of MGM's Andy Hardy series had been invaded by Reds, familiar only because of their frequent resemblance to the traditional gangsters of the thirties and forties. You almost wondered where Mickey Rooney was in our time of national need, until you remembered that women, not politics, were the continuing threat to his innocence.

The emphasis on American investigatory naïveté in the face of Communist infiltration reached proportions in *Walk a Crooked Mile* (1948) which outraged even J. Edgar Hoover, a man not usually noted for his critical scrutiny of film. One of the earliest anti-Communist flicks, it depicted a murderous spy escaping FBI surveillance by disguising himself as a clergyman. More astonishing was *The Whip Hand* (1951) in which Soviet agents successfully constructed a laboratory for developing germ warfare in a New England village. Perhaps to those who believed, with McCarthy, that Owen Lattimore was the top Russian spy in the country the movie was a credible reflection of their most morbid intuition.

Fortunately, the screen role of the FBI more characteristically reminded us that the federal government could move effectively against the threat of Soviet espionage. An FBI agent was instrumental in working a change in the conscience of Robert Walker, and, after his death, in consoling his parents in *My Son John*. Undercover agent Matt Cvetic was portrayed by Frank Lovejoy in *I Was a Communist for the FBI* (1951), a film dramatizing the successful, if dangerous, penetration of party apparatus by federal counterspies. The characterization was sufficiently popular to reappear on television in 1953 as "I Led Three Lives" with Richard Carlson as real-life agent Herbert Philbrick.

The most persuasive of the FBI cycle was easily Louis de Rochemont's production *Walk East on Beacon* (1952)— based loosely on the actual case of British spy Klaus Fuchs. In addition to de Rochemont's familiar documentary handling of the details of federal investigation, the film was almost alone in suggesting historically credible reasons for the international appeal of communism. The blackmailed scientist, whose protection is the job of FBI agent George Murphy, got involved with the Communists at Buchenwald where he "was only fighting Hitler." A cabbie joined the party during the Depression but found it was "like waking up married to a woman you hate." Active Communists are shown to be complexly different: a reluctantly fanatical spy whose failure results in his ambiguous punishment, a repressed couple with the look of an ascetic idealism in their pinched faces, a cynical bureaucratic leader, etc.

Most publicized of the anti-Communist films was the wordless tour de force, *The Thief* (1952), from the inventive team of Russell Rouse and Clarence Greene. Ray Milland withstood the unspoken invitations of his rooming-house neighbor, Rita Gam, while sweating out exposure of his illegal microfilming of government documents from the Atomic Energy Commission. The movie stretched the silent secret world of the spy well beyond private anguish into somnolent repetition. But the idea that even seedy boarding houses con-' tained possible encounters with lovely ladies in less than concealing bathrobes gave Milland's mission a romantic self-denial rare in other screen Communists. Commies, we learned, don't even get their ashes hauled.

The classic of the genre was so outrageously sanctimonious that it wrote in a part for God, placing him on a planet usually inhabited by unruly mutants. In *Red Planet Mars* (1952) a scientist contacts Mars and transmits to earth the accumulated wisdom of a society so advanced in technology that inhabitants live to a graceful three hundred years of age. Earth undergoes a miraculous religious revival in which a secret sect overthrows the Communist regime of Russia. It seems they kept their Christian fervor alive listening to Voice of America. Popular wish fulfillment had outdone McCarthy by directly enlisting God in the battle against the Red menace.

No one knows how, or if, these films influenced the election of 1952, or in what exact ways they contributed to the fearful and oppressive atmosphere of the early fifties. The mystery of the movies is that even after such solemn work as the Payne studies in the thirties we know precious little about the part films play in activating our national myths. Certainly, traditional fear of intellectuals, foreigners, and radicals was fed by the multiple portraits of each in the anti-Communist films. The ambiguity of Korea had produced an edginess in the country not consistent with the proud pioneer spirit so recently retested in that other war, that simpler war, already receding from memory into a simpler past. In Wisconsin reporters in the street asked passersby for signatures to the preamble of the Declaration of Independence. Over a hundred people read the document but only one was willing to affirm it with his signature. Most of the others regarded it as too radical. Our mothers were packing us off to college with instructions not to join anything, unless it had a Greek name and a secret handshake which Dad remembered.

The Eisenhower Era was upon us with its tone indelibly stamped from the first day onward. Aaron Copland's *A Lincoln Portrait* was dropped from the Inaugural Concert when a congressman decided it was "un-American." And at the Inaugural Reception Adolphe Menjou snubbed the Soviet Ambassador, no doubt courageously saving the movie industry from further infection. Ilka Chase, as the gossip columnist in *The Big Knife* (1955), reminded Jack Palance, "You used to believe in the New Deal, or the Fair Deal, or some deal. What do you believe in now?" And Palance, as a sold-out liberal, answered, "I believe in . . . rare roast beef and good scripts." The sentiment was an echo in the private sector of an administration whose Secretary of Defense could blandly announce, "What's good for General Motors is good for the country."

The anti-Communist films weren't good business for Hollywood, but the blacklist was. The Hollywood Ten were out of jail now, some of them returning to employment in an underground market which denied them screen credit and forced them to work for wages far below their pre-blacklist scale. Work was available abroad, too, under similar conditions. But there was a problem in getting there. In 1953 the State Department determined that it would "not be in the best interests of the United States" for Ring Lardner Jr. to travel to Europe. Sympathy for the Ten, especially in the literary community, was not especially high. In his mid-fifties book, *Part of Our Time,* Murray Kempton wrote that most blacklisted writers were little more than hacks for whom "the Comintern was a musical and Spain the Rose Bowl." Even John Howard Lawson's script for *Blockade* (1938), a film about the Spanish Civil War, was so diffuse that Lillian Hellman couldn't tell what side it was on. And neither could the D.A.R. "It is one of the myths of the fifties," Kempton wrote, "that communism in the thirties had a special attraction for the best talents."

Not all the blacklisted talent found ready work in the underground. Ned Young became a bartender. Alvah Bessie went to work for the hungry i, a nightclub in San Francisco. Albert Maltz went to Mexico to write a novel. Samuel Ornitz died of cancer and J. Edward Bromberg of a heart attack. Lionel Stander, in his belated HUAC appearance, was as helpful as a lighted firecracker.

And Herbert Biberman set out to make an independent film. Production on *Salt of the Earth* (1954) began in 1951 when Michael Wilson completed a screenplay about a miners' strike in which the women of the community replace the men on the picket lines when their husbands are faced with a legal injunction. From the beginning there was trouble. Few people in the industry wanted to risk the blacklist by working on a project controlled by people already blacklisted. Vigilante elements in Silver City, New Mexico, where location shooting took place, impeded production with harassment ranging from refusal of access to public streets to threats of armed raids against the company. Columnist Victor Riesel implied there was something sinister in all those Communists assembled so close to the atomic testing grounds at Los Alamos—shades of *The Whip Hand* in the national skull! Congressman Donald Jackson swore "to do everything in my power to prevent the showing of this Communist-made film in the theaters of America." And Howard Hughes in a letter to Jackson spelled out procedures by which film technicians could prevent the completion of any picture.

Despite deportation of its Mexican star and the furtive patience required to get the film processed, *Salt of the Earth* was ready for a world premiere in New York on March 14, 1954. Film critic Otis L. Guernsey showed up three hours early just to check on how well things were going. He wanted to be on hand if there was any trouble. His paper, the New York *Herald Tribune*, was especially interested in seeing that the film had every chance for uninterrupted public exhibition. The concern was warranted. A few months later an American Legion official attempted to discourage its booking in Chicago. He wrote the management of the Cinema Annex Theater that the movie was "an endeavor on the part of the Communistic elements to produce the greatest Communist propaganda picture ever developed in the United States of America." In Detroit all doors closed to the film.

When I caught up with *Salt of the Earth* in Los Angeles, I was still in high school. Fashionable Westwood Village, now one of the country's prime locations for first-run exposure— where *The Godfather* (1972) did nearly a quarter million in its initial week in just one of the nine theaters with fourteen separate auditoriums—was, in those days, a quiet gateway to UCLA. There were only three movie houses, and the last show in any of them put you on the deserted streets long before midnight. Once a year they still blocked off Westwood Boulevard for homecoming floats. And the closest thing to political protest was a mock funeral organized by David McReynolds to symbolize the death of the student newspaper as it passed under tougher administration guidelines intended to check intemperate remarks about the Eisenhower euphoria. Most people thought the weird procession with its garish coffin was a misguided advertisement for one of those European dramas occasionally produced by the Theater Arts Department. The entourage of students momentarily impeded traffic moving through the campus toward Sunset Boulevard and the entrance to Bel Air north of the university. Needless to say, *Salt of the Earth* wasn't booked in Westwood in 1954.

The word on the film was fierce. Supposedly it would convert you to communism faster than salty popcorn would to Coca-Cola. Brainwashing was much in the news. Defectors in the Korean War amazingly had denounced the United States. In *Assignment—Paris* (1952) Dana Andrews, as a newsman, had returned from Budapest a completely zonked potato. The Communists had done something to him with drugs and strobe lights. Going to *Salt of the Earth* was potentially dangerous, too. We were warned to park blocks from the Los Angeles theater because FBI men were taking down license plate numbers in the lot next to the movie. Even then there was the risk an undercover agent would film the audience through a cutout in the stage curtain.

High school counselors made it clear to those of us headed for college that many professions—law, medicine, teaching—required records pure as driven snow. On May 27 a special three-member Personnel Security Board of the Atomic Energy Commission had determined that Dr. J. Robert Oppenheimer was a security risk who should be denied top federal clearance. Nobel Prize winner Dr. Harold Urey worried about the effect of the decision on talented young people. He wondered if they wouldn't conclude it was too risky to enter government research work in sensitive areas, predicting that "many times a young man will decide to go to Standard Oil instead of the Atomic Energy Commission." If a distinguished scientist like Oppenheimer was fair game, why should we risk J. Edgar Hoover's shit list for a movie? Past associations, however casual, had a way of returning to ruin careers.

In a way I was disappointed with *Salt of the Earth*. I wasn't corrupted, and I couldn't see how anyone else could be either. If Hoover's men were in the crowd they were disguised as middle-aged Jewish radicals. The audience was chummier than I was used to at the Fox Westwood. Old friends clasped each other. Some of the women wore sandals and peasant shawls, their faces as severely intellectual as Jo Davidson's bust of Gertrude Stein. A beautiful girl my age was in Indian braids, but it was a little early in the decade for the Kerouac people to be out in large numbers. In the lobby that night was a shared political and cultural past which I could only guess at from the inadequate supplements I made to the bland version of white Protestant American history taught in high school.

The film, itself, reminded me of the proletarian fiction of Jack Conroy and William Cunningham recently discovered despite the fact that Herman Wouk was the direction in American fiction approved by my teachers. It was pro-union, of course, with touching and sentimental portrayals of the Mexican-American strikers strengthened by faces obviously more familiar with mining than motion picture cameras. Representatives of law and order were mean-spirited bigots who sneered about the proper way of addressing a white man, individuals as used to crushing the human spirit as they were to breaking an egg for breakfast, and as indifferent. It was an outsider's view of American society, but one familiar in American literature at least as far back as Melville's *White Jacket*. The shock was to see it on the screen. In 1954. But even there the only ones who could have worried about its effect on the state of the nation were men brought up exclusively on pieties learned at the knee of Louis B. Mayer.

Politically engaged films, particularly from the left, have never been popular, and especially not in the earlier fifties. But 1954 proved a transitional year in several ways that had immediate effect on the movies we saw. Eisenhower had concluded the Korean War, however ambiguously. And McCarthy's image was showing more than a little tarnish. In early 1953 he sent his dynamic duo of Roy Cohn and G. David Schine to Europe scouting for Communist propaganda in American overseas libraries. Schine, a close friend of Cohn's, was the latest addition to McCarthy's staff, signing on as a specialist in international communism. His claim to expertise consisted of a monograph published by his family for circulation in its hotel rooms. In it Schine confused Stalin with Trotsky, Marx with Lenin, and incorrectly identified the dates of both the Russian Revolution and the founding of the Communist party. A London columnist warned the duo that the American Library in London contained a book on wines with a suspiciously long section on the red ones. Cohn got a chuckle out of the joke, but still the two came home demanding the removal from overseas shelves of the detective novels of Dashiell Hammett. Even Eisenhower objected that he found nothing subversive in *The Maltese Falcon.*

Editorial ridicule alone never could have halted McCarthy. The image of him which emerged in newspapers was too abstract, his victims too easily forgotten in the haze of subsequent controversy and litigation. On March 9, 1954, Edward R. Murrow, on "See It Now," pinned McCarthy into the national imagination with film clips of the senator at work. On the small screen, McCarthy's outsize theatrics invaded the living room in ominous disproportion. His mannerisms, in these early days before cosmetic sensitivity to television imagery was widespread, immediately placed him in a recognizable tradition of B movie villains. It was all there: the sepulchral voice, beady eyes, unshaveable jowls above the permanently rumpled blue suit, and, most of all, the nervous laugh, at times like a manic tic—all details familiar to the television audience from a million collective hours of old bad movies.

McCarthy's rebuttal to Murrow only further exposed these characteristics, and in smearing the popular newsman revealed to millions the indiscriminate nature of his attacks. By summer the scene was set for the trial by television—the Army–McCarthy Hearings. The military's pixieish New England lawyer, Joseph Welch, successfully needled Cohn and McCarthy into traps of self-exposure culminating in McCarthy's merciless ambush of one of Welch's young colleagues, a man not even present at the hearings. Welch summarized the nation's feelings in an eloquent moment in television history: "Until this moment, Senator, I think I never really gauged your cruelty or your recklessness. . . .

CONTINENTAL DISTRIBUTING INC.
Senator McCarthy as he appeared on television screens during the Army-McCarthy Hearings in 1954. His bumptious style was more suitable to the late show villeins who followed the televised Hearings in many locations. Other man is Roy Cohn; chief counsel for the Senator's Committee, he later wrote a sympathetic insider's book about McCarthy.

Have you no sense of decency, sir, at long last? Have you left no sense of decency?" The censorial action of the Senate later in the year, although a rare historical event, was anti-climactic.

Television destroyed the unphotogenic McCarthy by framing him in a sinister tradition of villainy which he unknowingly accommodated. By contrast, Welch entered public mythology as the puckish custodian of common sense and gentle reason, a role which easily passed from reality to celluloid in Otto Preminger's *Anatomy of a Murder* (1959), wherein Welch played a judge playing himself.

The cycle of anti-Communist films almost exactly coincided with the period immediately following the first HUAC Hollywood hearings in 1947 and the Senate rebuke of McCarthy in late 1954. From the peak dozen films produced in 1952, the number dropped to five in 1953, even fewer in 1954.

After that there were only stragglers like *A Bullet for Joey* (1955) with Edward G. Robinson erasing any lingering doubts about his patriotic contempt for communism, and *The Fearmakers* (1958) with sorely used Dana Andrews discovering that the Sons of the Patriotic Pioneers, a group opposed to atomic warfare, is actually a Commie front promoted by his own ad agency. But the conviction was ebbing. In *Shack Out on 101* (1955) Frank Lovejoy, as a university physicist, pompously declaims, "While we were watching television and filling our freezers, they've come out of the jungle. . . . They even look like us. They've learned to dress like us and talk like us." But the threat seemed overstated when applied to Lee Marvin as "Slob," a short-order cook who deals in microfilmed secrets when not comparing his hairy legs to those of Keenan Wynn in a moronic beauty contest easily won by Terry Moore with a quick flash for the boys in the front row.

Films dealing with communism in the later fifties were more complex, even ambiguous, in their handling of the theme. The difference was evident almost immediately with the decline of McCarthy as a powerful public figure. Mark Robson's *Trial* (1955) detailed the party exploitation of a sensational murder trial involving a Mexican-American, one of the few films to trace the ideological gambits of Communist strategy with any credibility.

In 1956 only one anti-Communist film was made, Owen Crump's allegorical *The River Changes* produced in Germany for Warners. For the first time that year the industry released a film openly contemptuous of witch-hunts and book burnings. Deep thinkers had seen a symbolic comment on the Hollywood Ten in Carl Foreman's script for *High Noon* (1952), just as unfriendly witnesses saw in Elia Kazan's *On the Waterfront* (1954) a covert reply to their contempt for informers. But this was inside stuff, private messages, if such they were, between opposed camps within the film community. Daniel Taradash's *Storm Center* (1956) was in front an attack on the inquisitorial methods of HUAC.

Bette Davis, as a widowed librarian, resists the efforts of the town council to remove the book *The Communist Dream* from library shelves. The council's chief inquisitor, Brian Keith, recites her past membership in Communist front groups and charges her with being a dupe. But she refuses to back down and is fired. An impressionable boy, hearing that his friend, Davis, is actually a "Red" who keeps secret, evil books in the library, sets the building on fire in a vivid, if melodramatic, reminder of the aberrations we had produced in ourselves in the repressive atmosphere of recent years. The Legion of Decency labeled the film "propaganda," but the D.A.R. approved its condemnation of book burners. Maybe old and predictable allegiances were breaking up a little.

The next year Hollywood followed Broadway's lead in safely joking about Cold War relations with Russia in Cole

COLUMBIA
Storm Center: Library goes up in flames, symbolizing the repressive tendencies kindled by various witch hunts of the period. Harry Cohn didn't like the film, but let director Daniel Taradash make it anyway.

Porter's musical remake of *Ninotchka* (1939)—*Silk Stockings* (1957). Cyd Charisse was the most attractive screen Communist of the decade and she was converted to our side by the affable and ageless Fred Astaire, as well as by the erotic allure of Western fashions, symbolized in a dance frequently cut from television because of its sizzle. The abortive Hungarian Revolution of 1956, in addition to such a topical programmer as *The Beast of Budapest* (1958), produced a sympathetic portrait of a Communist officer, a man even capable of love, an emotion repeatedly proscribed for Reds in early fifties films: Yul Brynner in Anatole Litvak's *The Journey* (1959).

Samuel Fuller, who had treated Communist agents in the gangster format in *Pickup on South Street* (1953), discovered the Vietnam war for us in *China Gate* (1957). The film even preshadows the domino theory used to justify subsequent American intervention when the French vacated. But the most complex and ironically disturbing of all the decade's efforts to deal with communism was the much lambasted and unpopular film of Joseph L. Mankiewicz—*The Quiet American* (1958).

Also concerned with the Vietnam war during its French phase, it brought the cinema image of American innocence full cycle from the deb mentality of Elizabeth Taylor in *Conspirator* to the ambiguous capitalist ethic of businessman Audie Murphy. The bland Murphy, with his dog, Duke, comes to Saigon with the apparent notion that most international problems can be solved by a sudden injection of good old American enterprise. Michael Redgrave, as a cynical British journalist who has followed the Indochina war to the point of nausea, is simultaneously contemptuous of and threatened by Murphy's presence. They become rivals for a Vietnamese girl who has been the reporter's mistress, although Murphy is as shocked as a backwoods preacher to learn the girl was formerly a hooker. Redgrave lies and cheats

The Quiet American: Audie Murphy and Michael Redgrave in unpopular early film about American innocence and European duplicity in Vietnam. Fifties audience had trouble working up interest about obscure events in a country whose geography was as unpronounceable as its politics was convoluted.

to retain her affection, and when confronted by Murphy's knowledge of his deceit can only make a cruel joke of it: "European duplicity—we have to make up for lack of supplies."

So corrupted is the British journalist that he allows a Communist to convince him that Murphy is actually responsible for an explosion in the milk bar of a hotel. He consigns Murphy to certain assassination even after concluding that he is "one of the most truly innocent people" he's ever known. After Murphy is murdered, a French police inspector, Claude Dauphin, tells Redgrave the Communists manipulated him and "made a bloody fool out of you." The journalist even loses the Vietnamese girl, who rejects him as a man whose lack of commitment has become monstrous. The danger in *The Quiet American* is not so much the expected Communist treachery as it is European decadence and absence of resolve. The *Daily Variety* reviewer, as puzzled as any over the then obscure political implications of Vietnam, observed accurately, "There are likely to be an awful lot of people who'll come out of this film saying 'Who gives a damn?' " Clearly, it was a remote subject of no possible consequence to film fans of the fifties.

Among the Academy Awards for 1956 was an Oscar for the best screen story given to Robert Rich for the King Brothers' production *The Brave One*. Rich wasn't present to accept the award, hardly a keen disappointment to the assembled celebrities since nobody in the industry had ever heard of him. He had no prior credits and no listing in either the *Motion Picture Almanac* or the *Film Daily Year Book*. In fact, Rich only existed as a pseudonym for blacklisted Dalton Trumbo, one of the Hollywood Ten. The next year Pierre Boulle's screenplay for *The Bridge on the River Kwai* (1957) was honored with an Oscar by the Academy. Boulle had written the novel on which the movie was based, but his film credit was only another smoke screen intended to conceal Hollywood's conscience from itself. Insiders knew Carl Foreman and Michael Wilson, both blacklisted, were the real authors of the screenplay.

In 1958 I went to a Beverly Hills theater to see a first-run showing of Stanley Kramer's *The Defiant Ones* (1958). As the credits flashed onto the screen, I was surprised to hear a ripple of vigorous applause at the appearance of the names of the writers. The screenplay was by Nathan E. Douglas and Harold Jacob Smith. Years later, I learned that Nathan E. Douglas was the pseudonym of blacklisted actor/writer Ned Young, and that the applause that night was recognition among insiders that Kramer had defied the blacklist. The action rolling under the opening titles depicted two truck drivers and was so arranged that the writing credits appeared under a close-up of the faces of both men. There for all to see, for all who *could* see, was the name Nathan E. Douglas directly under a face many in the industry recognized as that of blacklisted Ned Young. It was an inside shot, a brazen sign of contempt which punctured the conventions of subterfuge even as it pretended to subscribe to them.

Early the next year the Academy rescinded its proscription on awards to ex-Communists and unfriendly congressional witnesses. Four days later on a Los Angeles television station Dalton Trumbo revealed for the first time publicly that, indeed, he was the notorious Robert Rich of Oscar fame. The blacklist, he supposed, had not been so bad, after all. At least he had been able to take credit for any good movie whose authorship was doubtful, while denying vehemently association with all of the stiffs he had written pseudonymously—such as his notable work as Sally Stubblefield on *The Green-Eyed Blonde* (1957).

Despite grumblings from the American Legion, Universal, although not required to by contract, decided to issue *Spartacus* (1960) identifying Trumbo as the screenwriter. In January of 1960 Otto Preminger openly announced Trumbo's employment as screenwriter on his next picture, *Exodus* (1960), for United Artists. Again the Legion fulminated. In March Frank Sinatra hired Albert Maltz, another of the Ten who had been blacklisted since 1947, to write the screenplay of *The Execution of Private Slovik* based on the book of that title by William Bradford Huie. The Legion, the Hearst papers, and Hedda Hopper formed a triumvirate in shrill disapproval. Sinatra backed down, canceling the film as Hopper said he should for the good of the country. Ironically, the picture both he and Maltz wanted to make about the only American soldier executed for cowardice in World War

II was a defense of the military establishment—in contrast to Huie's sympathetic view of Slovik as a scapegoat.

Entering the sixties the blacklist was easing, the climate changing. New energies were forming, and the old watchdogs of public morality sniffed the scent in the strangest places. William Mooring, film reviewer for the Brooklyn *Tablet,* detected propaganda for "peaceful co-existence" in the innocuous Danny Kaye picture *Me and the Colonel* (1958). The *American Mercury*, in its dying days as the ritual voice of right-wing America, urged its readers to adopt an eight-point program for uncovering and policing subversive content in films. "Above all," it warned, "Hollywood wants its customers . . . to remain lethargic and receptive to its propaganda." But then, as I. F. Stone noted in *The Haunted Fifties*, there will always be among us men, who, if told the President was seen riding a broomstick over the White House, will never believe the sworn testimony of his wife that he was at the time home in bed reading a Western.

3

There's an Ecdysiast in My Popcorn

I always thought it was the glasses. They pinched the rim of your ear, left a red mark on the bridge of your nose, and smelled faintly of suspicious origin in a chemistry laboratory. People complained of headaches and eyestrain. From certain angles in the theater inevitable distortion of the image occurred. I remember Biff Elliott as the 3-D Mike Hammer in *I, the Jury* (1953) shrinking down to a shrill pipsqueak as he drifted from the center of the screen to either side. Occasionally, the supply of glasses suddenly ran out, leaving a few dozen customers milling around waiting for extras to arrive from another part of town. Younger film fans caught in this circumstance were likely to take direct action. A friend borrowed his date's lipstick, went into the john, and in bold red letters used the mirror to advertise a special service performed by the feminine star of the picture he wasn't properly equipped to see. Then he demanded his money back from a manager who was already babbling to himself behind the candy counter. Yes, the glasses were a lot of trouble.

As early as 1951 exhibitors were promised that 3-D was on the way. "We are closer to this than most people realize. If we could just get over the hurdle of Polaroid glasses," Leon

J. Bamberger, an RKO sales manager, told a gathering of
New England theater owners. Earlier that year Milton Gunzburg and his brother, Julian, formed the Natural Vision
Corporation, but their attempt to sell the major studios on
their stereoscopic process wasn't successful. Columbia turned
it down. At Fox, Darryl F. Zanuck said nothing requiring
glasses could succeed. Paramount president Adolph Zukor,
at seventy-eight, was old enough to remember the stereoscopic cine-camera patented in 1889 by William Friese-Greene
and Mortimer Evans. It failed to give an adequate illusion
of movement. Paramount also turned down the Gunzburgs.
MGM, where John Arnold, chief of the camera department,
had worked privately with 3-D for thirty-five years, took an
option but allowed it to lapse.

Milton Gunzburg dejectedly watched the trial footage of
California hot rods he had prepared with his new camera
and wondered if anyone other than bedazzled friends and
querulous executives would ever get to cringe at objects apparently emerging from the screen with the audience as their
targets. And then one day Arch Oboler called on him. A radio
dramatist only lately diverted to movies with the extinction
of his old medium, Oboler told Gunzburg he wanted to use
Natural Vision for a feature-length film. Unfortunately, Oboler's previous movie, *Five* (1951), had not been financially
successful and so there was the difficult question of money.

For *Bwana Devil* (1952) Oboler invested ten thousand
dollars of his own, raising the rest outside the indifferent industry which already had rejected the commercial potential
of Gunzburg's process. In December of 1952, without a distributor, Oboler opened the first 3-D feature at two Paramount theaters in Los Angeles. *Bwana Devil* brought in a
stunning one hundred fifty-four thousand dollars in its first
week. A distributor followed within a month. United Artists
paid Oboler five hundred thousand dollars outright, retained
the next half million in revenues, and agreed to pay Oboler

a subsequent one and a quarter million dollars before returning to the till itself. And nobody thought UA had struck a
bad bargain out of the deal.

The boom was on. "The most frenzied boom since the
birth of sound," puffed a *Life* headline in February of 1953.
Warners hired Gunzburg as it attempted to rush *House
of Wax* (1953) out as the first 3-D film from a major
studio. Polaroid granted Natural Vision an exclusive one-
year contract to distribute the necessary cardboard glasses.
The Gunzburgs sold one hundred million to exhibitors at ten
cents apiece. Polaroid stock rose 30 percent in a matter of
weeks. About the troublesome glasses Jack Warner predicted,
"We are convinced that the public will wear such viewers as
effortlessly as they wear wristwatches or carry fountain pens."
Producer William Thomas was even more euphoric in his
expectations for the audience. "They'll wear toilet seats
around their necks if you give 'em what they want to see,"
he said. His production of *Sangaree* (1953) at Paramount
was scrapped after twelve days of shooting to be resumed in
3-D with an added budget of four hundred thousand dollars.
"Artists who are great in two dimensions will be even greater
with a third!" enthused a Paramount executive. A variation
on that theme apparently occurred simultaneously to Sol
Lesser and Howard Hughes. Both signed ecdysiast Lili St.
Cyr for 3-D films.

At Warners the Gunzburg camera was lugged from set to
set in a padlocked trunk, carefully guarded from spies by
armed studio police during lunch breaks. Despite this precau-
tion, Columbia nipped Warners by three days to be the first
studio to complete a 3-D production. Director Lew Landers
finished *Man in the Dark* (1953) in just eleven days. Somebody asked production chief Jerry Wald about the longevity
of the new gimmick. Wald replied, "We'll throw things at the
public until they start throwing them back!"

Allied Artists assigned famed designer William Cameron

Menzies to direct *The Maze* (1953). At Universal technicians worked twenty hours a day to develop a new camera for the studio's first 3-D film, *It Came From Outer Space* (1953). The experienced John Arnold at MGM was able to train a crew and build equipment in only eighteen days after the studio decided to get its feet wet. But MGM, Fox, and RKO all hedged by filming their initial 3-D pictures so that they could be projected flat as well. And, meanwhile, United Artists, with the lone available product, watched as nearly every UA record fell with each engagement of *Bwana Devil*.

By March the action reached a point where *Film Daily*, a trade paper, introduced a new column, the "3-D Bulletin Board," just to keep the industry in touch with its own hysteria. In April the two-thousand-seat Colisseum Theater in San Francisco became the first movie house to play 3-D films exclusively. A restaurant nearby offered "3-D chili." In early summer Three Dimensional Publications of Boston published a twenty-four-page *I Love Lucy* magazine with Polaroid glasses inserted to make the pictures jump to life. The monthly *Three Dimension Entertainment World* followed, but the first shipment to Los Angeles arrived without glasses, leaving news vendors cross-eyed trying to figure out the unfocused images of the photographs inside. A midwestern minister preached a sermon on "Prayer—the Third Dimension," while in London Canterbury's "Red Dean," the Very Reverend Dr. Hewlett Johnson, curbed our national pride by reminding us that "the Americans have cribbed 3-D from the Russians." But a crueler remark appeared in Ed Sullivan's syndicated column, which reported that sophisticated New Yorkers were boycotting 3-D because they didn't like the odor of the plastic glasses.

By the summer of 1953, only six months after Oboler first planted the African veld in Paramount's balconies, the greatest boom since sound began to appear as dubious an investment as underwater land in Florida in the twenties. Audiences were

tiring of weekly impalements almost as quickly as prop de-
partments ran out of new implements on which to impale
them. In its June cover story on the screen's new dimensions,
Time asked, "Had Hollywood really done more than recapture the public's attention by slapping it in the face?" Reactions from exhibitors were somewhat less rhetorical. By
August *Film Daily* was passing along their open hostility.
"Take it from circuit executives, the bloom is off the 3-D
rose. . . . And there's a growing feeling that the industry
was not exactly smart in its mad scramble for a quick 3-D
buck."

By October Chicago's Great States Circuit announced it
would no longer exhibit films in three-dimension. Fox's *In-
ferno* (1953), RKO's *Second Chance* (1953), and Allied
Artists' *The Maze*, each the first 3-D film of its respective
studio, were all exhibited flat. Robert L. Lippert, whose
theater chain operated right in the industry's backyard, announced, "Very definitely 3-D is dead!" Warners, which had
once expected to make most of its films in Natural Vision, released Alfred Hitchcock's *Dial M For Murder* (1954) in
two versions. Most people saw it flat. Pictures originally announced as 3-D projects were regularly released for standard
projection, sometimes with disastrous results. *Top Banana*
(1954) was intended as a filmed stage play observing pro-
scenium conventions complete with curtain breaks throughout.
Without the novelty of 3-D it looked like an opulent version
of the sort of burlesque films Samuel Cummins had produced
a few years earlier for the specialty houses. At least *Red
Garters* (1954), initially touted as the first grand-scale musical in 3-D, retained a wild sense of color, imaginative sets,
and some amusing moments spoofing Westerns.

In the summer of 1954 the tag ends of the stereoscopic
revolution were reaching the screen. By now they were mostly
science fiction and horror films like *Creature from the Black
Lagoon* (1954) and *Gog* (1954). Or *The Mad Magician*

(1954), in which a new missile to project at the audience was finally discovered—a severed head. The popular Creature made a final 3-D appearance in the summer of 1955 in *Revenge of the Creature.* Reportedly it wowed them in Denver. Most everybody else saw it flat.

In those months of golden promise, early in 1953, a Viennese inventor toured New York announcing that he had solved the problem of the Polaroid glasses. His new screen contained all the optical components necessary for three-dimensional effect. It was a wonderful screen capable of converting ordinary pictures into 3-D. It produced nine times the light of the standard screen. "It shimmers, it is alive!" he told various reporters and potential financial backers. At the moment he had to fly back to Vienna for the first installation at the end of April, but he would return in the fall. When he arrived in New York in September none of his anticipated investors met him at the airport.

Despite 3-D the box-office returns for 1953 were the worst in the continuing decline since the end of the war, dropping from the peak 1.7 billion of 1946 to under 1.2 billion. Even Cinerama, the other spectacular innovation of 1952, obviously was not going to slow the downward drift. Previewed for exhibitors and the press as early as 1950, Cinerama was front-page news in *The New York Times* when *This Is Cinerama* (1952) bowed to the public in October. Where 3-D achieved spectator intimacy by reproducing the effects of binocular vision, Cinerama accomplished a similar end by wrapping the viewer in a 145° screen, nearly duplicating the full 160° range of peripheral vision. So attuned was inward experience to this extended field of visual awareness that the roller coaster ride, rattled and bumped to the audience over six separately located speakers in the theater, nauseated some of the first nighters who rushed dizzily from their seats onto steadier ground near the drinking fountain.

Cinerama was an immediate sensation but rather exclusive in its possibilities. Projection required a gigantic curved screen as well as three separate projection booths. Cost of restructuring the few theaters sufficiently large to accommodate the process ranged from forty thousand to seventy-five thousand dollars, clearly limiting Cinerama to a few key cities throughout the country. However, the idea of sheer size was bound to prove fascinating to a community which remembered its greatest financial success to be *Gone With the Wind* (1939).

While Warners and Columbia hurtled into 3-D, Fox decided to commit itself to its own more economical version of the wide screen—CinemaScope. Late in 1952 Fox purchased a reduction lens from its French inventor Henri Chrétien. Screwed onto an ordinary movie camera, the lens squeezed a wider picture onto standard 35 mm. film. A compensating lens on the theater projector spread the picture out again onto a screen about twice as wide as traditional screens and a third smaller than Cinerama. Best of all, the cost for theater conversion to CinemaScope was between ten thousand and twenty-five thousand dollars, more than 3-D but considerably less than Cinerama.

Only cost had prevented the wide screen phenomenon from being exploited much earlier in motion picture history. Giant flicks had been around nearly as long as films in any size. At the Paris Exposition of 1900 Raoul Grimoin-Sanson introduced Cinéorama consisting of ten projectors and a huge circular screen, while down the road apiece the Lumière Brothers had a six-story screen so big it wouldn't fit into the building constructed to house it. In the twenties and thirties major American studios developed large screen processes with names like Magnascope, Realife, and Magnifilm. In the heart of the Depression, when the success of such novelties terrified exhibitors with the thought of costly restructuring, Adolph Zukor promised on behalf of the producers that nobody would make any more oversize films until things got better. Or much worse.

Early in 1953 Darryl F. Zanuck boldly announced that Fox was converting its entire production to CinemaScope. What about 3-D? the smart money asked. "Depth. We don't need depth . . . I have been supplying my own third dimension all my life. What we need is to open up, open up wide," said Zanuck. Within a few months Fox had succeeded in convincing some four thousand theaters to convert to the new process. *The Robe* (1953), a film already one month into production in standard size, was elected the first representative of the studio's new commitment. Rushes of *The Robe* in CinemaScope drew an enthusiastic if occasionally baffling response. When one exhibitor returned to home territory he was asked what the picture was about. "I don't know," he said, then, remembering a mind-boggling close-up of stony-faced Victor Mature, "I think it's about a guy with thirteen-foot lips."

Opening in September of 1953, *The Robe* was an instant success and within a short time second only to *Gone With the Wind* as Hollywood's top blockbuster. Fox's second CinemaScope feature, *How To Marry a Millionaire* (1953) with Marilyn Monroe, was no slouch, hauling in more than seven million in its first year of play. Warners and MGM made arrangements to use CinemaScope, and in late 1954 Paramount unveiled its own competing process with *White Christmas* (1954) in VistaVision. It took in six million in its first seven weeks. In the history of film only about one hundred pictures had grossed more than five million dollars prior to 1953. In the first year and a half of the CinemaScope era more than thirty films exceeded that figure, most of them wide screeners. By 1954 over 50 percent of all films were in color with nearly a quarter of all releases in jumbo size. At the end of 1955 thirteen thousand theaters were equipped to handle the new product. In fact, the deepies were so suc-

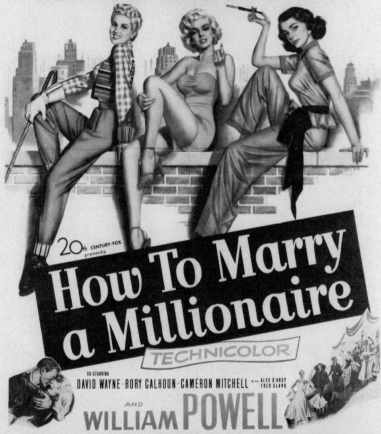

20TH CENTURY-FOX
How To Marry a Millionaire: War against 3-D glasses was part of early
CinemaScope advertising, but insipid three-dimensional films insured easy
victory for the wide screen as the dominant process for future movies.

cessful that studios decided to project their $330,000,000 backlog of unreleased flatties onto the new screens, even though there was a picture loss of about 25 percent at the top or bottom of the frame.

The early years of CinemaScope produced astonishing confusions in the relative size of things seen for the first time in monstrous close-up. In *Bus Stop* (1956) Marilyn Monroe's dialogue was punctuated with gigantic loops of saliva, while, for the less orthodontically inclined, the undulating bottom of Jayne Mansfield dominated *The Girl Can't Help It* (1956). Two-shots gave to conversation the intimacy of dialogue conducted across ranges of screen space appropriate for departing herds of cattle but impossibly wide for mere words. "Marilyn Monroe will have to lie down before the audience can get a good look at her," noted one film maker.

Cinematographers complained bitterly about the destruction of their work. Leon Shamroy told Charles Higham that CinemaScope "nearly drove me out of my mind . . . You got a stage play again, you put pictures back to the earliest sound days . . . it wrecked the art of film for a decade." Director George Seaton agreed, adding that to produce certain small and intimate stories in wide screen was as ludicrous "as staging a chess match in the Rose Bowl." George Stevens, a director noted for his visual acuity, said, "The question is whether you want a system of photography that pictures a boa constrictor to better advantage than a man." Ultimately the technical deficiencies were corrected and the full rich potential of cinematography reemerged integrated with the demands of the new screen sizes.

Perhaps the most disastrous result of CinemaScope was to push Hollywood into a frame of mind where its usual obsession with spectacle became inextricably linked to high-rolling gambles on increasingly more opulent, more expensive pictures. The mania for production values mounted until Jerry Lewis quipped, "At nine million *War and Peace* cost more

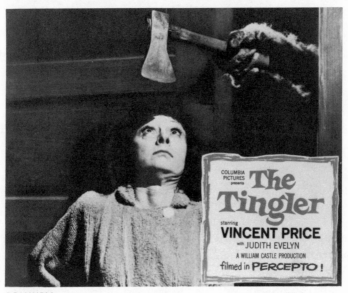

COLUMBIA
The Tingler: William Castle's Percepto was one of many carny hustles which failed to reverse the continued downtrend in movie attendance in the late fifties.

than the war itself did." For *The Roots of Heaven* (1958) Zanuck went to Africa to film the largest herd of elephants ever put on film. The terrain and heat nearly killed half his cast, and Eddie Albert had to be tied to his bed when sunstroke caused him to rave through the company announcing impending snow storms. But what scenic splendor, six hundred elephants following Trevor Howard to freedom. And there were nine hundred sick calls, a record for a crew of one hundred and twenty-five.

Economists now call the period 1954–56 the "Cinema-Scope rebound." But by 1958 the downward trend had resumed. What were Zanuck's six hundred elephants when around the corner John Wayne's Batjac Productions was literally reconstructing the nineteenth century by rebuilding the historical town of San Antonio for *The Alamo* (1960) at the cost of one million five? Despite the success of *The Bridge on the River Kwai*, Columbia reported a loss of four million dollars for 1958. Industry grosses dropped below the billion-dollar mark for the first time in eighteen years, a decline in revenues of nearly 30 percent in only twenty-four months. In September Spyros Skouras, president of Twentieth Century-Fox, told Walter Wanger, "*Cleopatra* was one of the best pictures we ever made. Just give me this over again and we'll make a lot of money." The rest, as they say, is history.

Writing in 1956 with belated enthusiasm for the undeveloped possibilities of 3-D, George Bluestone wondered if eventually the moviegoer doesn't turn "his attention from the flaming arrow back to the Apache who shot it." Not if the seat in which he's sitting has been wired to conduct an unexpected electric tickle up his backside, while a lady hired by Columbia faints two rows down during a key scene in William Castle's *The Tingler* (1959).

Some of the most endearing memories of the fifties are such technological remnants of the carny spirit as Hypnovista, HypnoVision, Psychorama, and Emergo. Hypnovista was nothing but a tedious thirteen-minute lecture on hypnotism in a prologue to *Horrors of the Black Museum* (1959). Producer Charles Bloch was more mysteriously ambitious. HypnoVision employed "techniques of applied psychology" to "cross the delta range of the brain wave cycles and so induce a receptive state." But nothing short of sodium pentothal could have adequately tranquilized audiences facing *The Hypnotic Eye* (1960) or most of the other movies trading on a scientific hype last seen in the formaldehyde jars of sideshows.

Psychorama exploited a current debate before the FCC and the National Association of Broadcasters over the use of subliminal advertising. In *My World Dies Screaming* (1958) horrific words and images were flashed onto the screen at the speed of $\frac{1}{50}$th of a second per impression. This was supposedly just long enough to prod an archetypal shudder from the subconscious. However chilling the technique in horror films, James Vicary of the Subliminal Projection Co. reported that correctly used it was a very useful way to stimulate an interest in popcorn at intermission. Iowa theater owner Harold Field concurred. In January of 1958 he had his best month in history using subliminal techniques to sell everything from soft drinks to next week's feature. In the summer the NAB banned from television all such exercises in mind manipulation.

Veteran thrillmaker William Castle was less indebted to the higher sciences for Emergo. In fact, it turned out to be nothing more than a squeaky luminous skeleton on a pulley which rattled out above the audience from a cubbyhole to the side of the screen. That is, if a harried theater manager wasn't too busy to remember the gimmick when the time for its appearance occurred in *House on Haunted Hill* (1959).

With Smell-O-Vision and AromaRama in the last year of the decade technical invention reached a desperate edge of self-parody. As in so many instances in Hollywood's creative past there was a race between competing interests to introduce intended odors into the movie experience. Unkind skeptics were quick to point out that old-fashioned stinkers had been around for years. Presumably Mike Todd Jr.'s *Scent of Mystery* (1959) and Walter Reade Jr.'s *Behind the Great Wall* (1959) would require a new vocabulary of olfactory esthetics. Reade promised on behalf of both processes that "you can be sure none of our smells will be objectionable."

If perfumed movies had a future, show biz speculation favored young Todd's Smell-O-Vision as the critical entry. Michael Todd Sr. had been interested in the project as early as 1954, shortly after General Electric introduced its own Smell-o-rama late the year before. Smell-o-rama was only a 3-D rose with scented puffs from an atomizer to accompany it. Still, the possibilities were evident. One of the photographers assembled for GE's exhibition said the experience opened his sinuses for the first time in a week.

Todd Jr. spent two million dollars on his picture. For three hundred thousand dollars Reade Jr. had picked up a European travelogue to which he added AromaRama in an obvious effort to tap interest in the smellies developed by Todd's publicity over a period of many months. Converting theaters for Smell-O-Vision in Los Angeles and Chicago cost about one hundred thousand dollars each, with over twenty of this invested in the forty odors alone. The scents—ranging from coffee and seafood to the villain's pipe—emerged from apparatus installed in the seats, with each odor hopefully wafted away by a special fan system before the next one entered the atmosphere.

The New Yorker's John McCarten wrote rather favorably of *Scent of Mystery*, notably restraining himself from the easy fame most memorably achieved in Henny Youngman's two-line review: "I didn't understand the picture. I had a cold." Other critics were impressed with a scene in which a man was crushed to death under wine casks while the audience was inundated in aromatic clouds of port. Sadly, I caught up with the film a few years too late, an unscented version playing in one of those all-night theaters famous for odors all its own. When I told the manager how great *Scent of Mystery* must have been in its original version, he looked puzzled for a minute. Then, just to show he was hip as any film buff, he shook his head. "Whattsa matter, kid, didn't you know 3-D went out years ago?"

4

Dark Streets and Dead Ends

The country was scared coming into the fifties. Winning the war proved psychologically easier than adjusting to the position of leadership in the tense post-atomic world. The national threat implicit in the Stalinization of Europe and Asia was symbolically recognized when Truman in 1946 ordered a loyalty oath for government employees. Three years later the nuclear gap closed as Russia detonated its first atomic bomb. The narrator of Merle Miller's novel *That Winter* caught the uneasy mood of impending disaster with his very first sentence: "We all drank too much that winter, some to forget the neuroses acquired in the war just ended, others in anticipation of those expected from the next. . . ."

Some of us were going underground, immediately and literally, digging in from bomb shelter instructions available in two-dollar booklets. The more affluent had choices ranging from thirteen-dollar foxhole kits to fifty-five-hundred-dollar subterranean suites with telephones, Geiger counters, and the last good wine out of a potentially devastated Europe. *The New Yorker* interviewed a Bronxville man who was arming his shelter with a Smith & Wesson .38 in practical anticipation of defending against invaders and looters from unprepared Manhattan.

Those with less apocalyptic imaginations nonetheless felt the chill of a strange new climate in the land. Early in 1951 William Poster wrote that "in the last three or four years the people of this country have been going through the most drastic change of mind in their history." America was entering a new era of cynicism born out of a widening popular recognition of the duplicity of international politics. At home journalists Jack Lait and Lee Mortimer wrote a series of increasingly sensational crime exposes—*New York Confidential, Washington Confidential, U.S.A. Confidential.* The authors saw the entire country made up of pimps and whores, many of whom, for the sake of old conventions, were temporarily disguised as local and national politicians. Corruption was everywhere. Lait and Mortimer renamed the Statue of Liberty the "Statue of Larceny." In *U.S.A. Confidential* they asserted that even Senator Estes Kefauver's Crime Commission was nothing but a political show-biz outgrowth of their own earlier work. Kefauver's book, *Crime in America,* was just a collection of "literary cribbings." But what could you expect in an America "becoming a land of manicured hermaphrodites, going the way of Rome"?

Only months after these stern pronouncements appeared, publisher James Harrison devoted the pages of his new *Confidential* magazine to detailing the Roman ways of the most famous celebrities in the country. With monthly sales near five million, *Confidential* became the best-selling newsstand magazine in publishing history. Television investigations, journalistic exposes, confidential reports—America was at the keyhole, shocked and breathless, and with the growing realization that most people lived inhibited and powerless lives psychic light-years from where the real action was taking place.

* * *

At the movies the paranoid note was particularly obvious. In 1947 John Garfield defiantly told the gangsters he had doubled-crossed in *Body and Soul* that they couldn't scare him because "everybody dies!" What a line! And it rightly earned the approval of gorgeous Lilli Palmer in the bargain, although we were left to conclude on our own what retribution he faced for winning the fight he was supposed to throw. "Walk slow and stay with the crowds," an inept Garfield was told four years later by a dying accomplice after they botched the robbery in *He Ran All the Way* (1951).

John Berry directed Garfield's last movie as if he were under an injunction to film the more dour implications of David Riesman's *The Lonely Crowd,* published only a year earlier. In the kitchen of one of those anonymous urban walk-ups with little light and less space, Garfield gives Shelley Winters and her family a history lesson about contemporary America. At gunpoint he demands they join him in a turkey dinner he has prepared. They refuse. What can happen to them in a crowded apartment in the center of a large city? Garfield shows them. He says he could murder them at the dinner table and nobody would notice or care about the shots. To prove his case he fires randomly and the only person who responds thinks it's a car backfiring. But Garfield doesn't kill them. He's neither a murderer nor a professional thief, only another victim of the urban paranoia which it has been his single accomplishment to communicate to Winters with such force that she shoots him dead.

The fearful city was conveyed with near-expressionist horror in Ted Tetzlaff's *The Window* (1949)—*film noir* at its darkest. Bobby Driscoll, accidentally overseeing a murder committed by Paul Stewart, must hide or be killed. Played out in dark rooms pulsating with the sound of the el, long shadowed stairwells, alleys, and condemned buildings with rotting timbers—*The Window* was a claustrophobic nightmare in which not even the police would believe or help you.

There were sunnier streets but an equally enveloping fear in the Russell Rouse–Clarence Greene *D.O.A.* (1950), the classic film of urban paranoia. Edmond O'Brien, already an inexplicable murder victim slowly dying from poisoning, searches the tourist traps of San Francisco for the identity of his killer. Since he doesn't know the motive, the suspects are equal to the number of people with whom he has come in contact in the last twenty-four hours. O'Brien is confronted with a city of potential killers, a Kafkaesque vision as oppressive as anything in the decade.

But there's plenty of competition ranging through every popular film genre from science fiction to the detective story —from the metaphorically brilliant *Invasion of the Body Snatchers* (1956) and *The Incredible Shrinking Man* (1957) to such driven creatures as Jack Palance in *Panic in the Streets* (1950), Arthur Franz in *The Sniper* (1952), Ralph Meeker in *Kiss Me Deadly* (1955), and Vince Edwards in *City of Fear* (1959). Even the police in *Slaughter on Tenth Avenue* (1957) have to deal with a little old lady afraid to walk her cat, Mittens, because, don't you know, enemy rays are always beamed at her.

As vaguely malevolent as the city was, the ambulatory psychotics on its daily streets were far more terrifying. In the forties crazies tended to be as obvious as a blinking neon sign. Cagney's Oedipal wigginess in *White Heat* (1949) was visible blocks away. But in the fifties psychic malignancy blended more ambiguously with the environment. Bogey in Nicholas Ray's beautifully ironic *In a Lonely Place* (1950) is a case in point. Only it isn't Bogey anymore, at least not the understated tough guy of *The Maltese Falcon* (1941) or *The Big Sleep* (1946), not even the murderer of *The Two Mrs. Carrolls* (1947) or the obsessive Dobbs of *The Treasure of the Sierra Madre* (1948). In *Lonely*

COLUMBIA
In a Lonely Place: Neurotically violent Bogart in Nicholas Ray's 1950 film confused filmgoers who were more comfortable with tough but lovable Bogey from such forties movies as *The Maltese Falcon.* Gloria Grahame is on the bed, where Bogart has thrown her in a characteristic burst of paranoid anger.

Place Bogart is a screenwriter falsely suspected of killing a hatcheck girl. Cleared by the testimony of Gloria Grahame he is slowly revealed as a man so uncontrollably violent as to be capable of murder at nearly any unsuspected moment. He is the sort of person you have a civilized dinner with one evening only to read the next morning that he has strangled a cabdriver over the matter of a tip.

The secret of the ambulatory psychotic is that he fools us by adjusting superficially to the life around him; the terror is that his real self may surface at any moment. As the witty but mad astrologer in *Whirlpool* (1950) Jose Ferrer easily bags Gene Tierney, almost convincing her that she's a murderess. Easygoing Robert Mitchum is so befuddled by Jean Simmons in *Angel Face* (1952) that he bids her farewell only to be conned into a suicidal auto ride which takes them both about twenty yards in reverse off a precipice at her father's place. Even dehumanized killers like Eli Wallach in *The Lineup* (1958) or Vince Edwards in *Murder By*

Contract (1958) are hard to spot unless they make a critical error. Edwards does daily chin-ups because in his profession you have to stay in shape, and Wallach is a nifty dresser who tries to improve himself by learning the subjunctive from his educated colleague, Robert Keith. As Keith says, "How many guys on street corners can say 'if I were you'?" Many fewer than crazies in button-down shirts apparently.

The chameleon psychotic can be anywhere, anyone, even his own mother in *Psycho* (1960). Criminal activity is equally omnipresent, the gradations between ethical business and corrupt practice shading away into a gray zone in which criminals look more like straights than the banker's son does. In *New York Confidential* (1955) Richard Conte is preoccupied with loyalty and respectability—the virtues of corporate life applied to the career of a rising young man in the syndicate. Lee J. Cobb in *On the Waterfront* is just a gruff father whose business occasionally requires that he nail the body of a dead *son* against the wall to reaffirm his patriarchal control of the family.

Film after film of the fifties extended the journalistic insights of Lait and Mortimer, subjecting virtually every geographical area of the country and most occupational groups to systematic expose—*Hoodlum Empire* (1952), *Kansas City Confidential* (1952), *The Miami Story* (1954), *New Orleans Uncensored* (1955), *Chicago Syndicate* (1955), *The Phenix City Story* (1955), *Inside Detroit* (1955), *The Houston Story* (1956), *Portland Expose* (1957), *The Case Against Brooklyn* (1958), and on and on. With corruption so widespread it was no surprise that the cops were repeatedly on the take in such films as *Kansas City Confidential, Rogue Cop* (1954), *Shield for Murder* (1954), and *Damn Citizen* (1958). Arthur Knight wasn't alone when he lamented in *Saturday Review*, "These aren't the cops we knew when I was a boy."

With crime continually depicted as a model of corporate

activity complete with board meetings and financial reports, the old-fashioned and outmoded loner gangs of *The Asphalt Jungle* (1950) and *The Killing* (1956) acquired the sympathetic charm of faded clippings from old newspapers. Elisha Cook Jr. was never going to make the big time, no matter how many promises he made to Marie Windsor. And when, in *Asphalt Jungle,* Sam Jaffe lingers too long in the juke joint watching the teen-age girl jive it for him, we know from his cryptic smile that he senses the arrival of a new age of which he is only a fast receding part. Even Orson Welles' intuitive but crooked cop in *Touch of Evil* (1958) is curiously sympathetic, a candy-bloated man caught out by a tape recorder and a trusted sidekick disillusioned into conspiracy against him.

If we had only movies by which to measure cultural change, those of the fifties would give us an image of an America darkly disturbed by its own cynical loss of in-

UNITED ARTISTS
The Killing: Despite careful planning and grotesque mask, Sterling Hayden fares no better in Stanley Kubrick's movie about a race track heist than he had six years earlier in John Huston's *The Asphalt Jungle.*

MGM
The Asphalt Jungle: Sam Jaffe gets sneak preview of decade's coming attractions as Helene Stanley performs pre-rock shimmy for him.

nocence, an America prey to fears more pervasive and intense than anything admitted to during the war years. From the HUAC 1947 hearings through Kefauver's 1955 Hollywood sojourn to the State Department's complaints about *Blackboard Jungle* (1955) and *On the Beach* (1959), the government intermittently objected to what they were doing to Old Glory out there on Crazy Coast. Eric Johnston, in the trusted voice of moderation, answered back, "America is growing up and the films must catch up."

But innocence dies hard, and not everyone is in agreement on what it means to grow up. An outraged spectator at Kefauver's 1955 investigation into sex and violence in films asked Jack Warner how many pictures he'd made in which women drank and smoked. Warner snapped back, "You must be living in the backwoods country, boy. Everybody's smoking and drinking now." Exactly. And the unasked next question was, What part does the screen play in producing controversial changes in social behavior, in modifying cultural attitudes toward significant national experience? According to exhibitors writing to the *Motion Picture Herald*, *The Wild One* (1954) was inflicting instant imitation on them. After eighty minutes with Brando, teen-agers hooded it up in the lobby, treating usherettes as if they were Mary Murphy waiting to be hustled off into the motorcycle darkness. It was fair warning to others about the more or less unpredictable magic involved in going to the movies.

I was fourteen when early in 1950 I saw a black woman kiss a white man on the screen for the first time. Only I think I missed it. You see, even to a fourteen-year-old, Jeanne Crain in *Pinky* was not, well, a black person. She wasn't even Lena Horne, the only black actress admitted to our middle-class white fantasies in those days. Like other stars of the forties Jeanne Crain projected over any role the cumulative image of her past performances. Who could be upset at Margie kissing William Lundigan? For me, the socially improving content of *Pinky* was simply filtered out by Fox's choice of casting a white actress in a black part. I remember faint puzzlement over Pinky's decision not to marry the northern doctor. Actually, it may not have been her decision. Miscegenation was proscribed by the Production Code until 1956.

As early as *Till the End of Time* (1946) Robert Mitchum and Guy Madison, as returning GI's, got into a beer brawl with self-styled patriot racists. After all, that was what the war had been all about—its most visceral lesson. Robert Ryan hadn't learned it in *Crossfire* (1947), and Gregory Peck found anti-Semitism still rampant when he passed himself off as Jewish in *Gentleman's Agreement*. MGM's *The Boy With Green Hair* (1948) safely distanced the problem of discrimination in fantasy, but the question "Would you like your sister to marry a boy with green hair?" clued hip audiences as to the real theme of the picture.

Stanley Kramer's independent production *Home of the*

Brave (1949) initiated a cycle of frank pictures about black Americans, among the earliest of which were *Lost Boundaries* (1949) and *Pinky.* Kramer's film was shot in seventeen days on a miniscule budget, and together with *Champion* (1949) established his position as a new force in Hollywood. *Pinky,* surprisingly, was Fox's top box-office attraction of the year.

The tougher films were yet to come, and the tensions to which they gave increasingly open expression were a considerable test of the adaptability of the new postwar audience everybody theorized about. People who had grown up on Mantan Moreland and Stepin Fetchit were prepared, perhaps, to allow the Negro porter of *Three for Bedroom C* (1952) to be a college graduate. They might even be attracted to the conventional heroics of *The Jackie Robinson Story* (1950) or *The Joe Louis Story* (1953). The race riots of *No Way Out* and *The Well* (1951) were another matter entirely.

20TH CENTURY-FOX
No Way Out: Doctors Stephen McNally and Sidney Poitier appear understandably concerned over the latter's treatment of racist patient Richard Widmark. The unpopularity of this Joseph L. Mankiewicz picture helped kill off the cycle of tough black films until much later in the decade.

Sidney Poitier was introduced in Joseph L. Mankiewicz's *No Way Out* as an intern unluckily the object of Richard Widmark's psychopathic hatred. The scathing dialogue flung such terms as *boogies, jigs, niggers, dinges, coons,* and *Sambos* at an audience accustomed to the more politely disguised racism of Mantan Moreland muttering "Feets do your thing" as he shuffled on out of trouble in a Charlie Chan flick. The pitched battle conducted in a junkyard under the eerie light from a flare had its only immediate screen precedent in newsreels of the 1943 Detroit race riot. An even less popular film was the Russell Rouse–Clarence Greene picture, *The Well*, in which a young black girl's disappearance sets off a racial disturbance in a small town. The state of our national innocence was well indicated in a Bosley Crowther *New York Times* review which concluded that the blacks in *The Well* were manifestly incapable of such hostility toward whites.

Black audiences of the early fifties were no more ready than whites to support films that dramatized repressed racial grievances. At the turn of the decade there were nearly seven hundred movie houses in the South and urban black belts of the North described by the trade as Negro theaters. A product entirely invisible to the white population played this black circuit. From Toddy Pictures and Negro Marches On came such films as *Harlem on Parade* (194?) and *Bronze Venus* (194?) with Lena Horne, *Mantan Runs for Mayor* (194?) with Mantan Moreland, *House Rent Party* (194?) with Pigmeat Markham, and countless other films more Uncle Tomish than anything produced for the mass audience in Hollywood. According to producer Ted Toddy, the black market simply wouldn't go for "heavy emotional drama." There was no *Super Fly* (1972) or *Shaft* (1971) for black audiences in the fifties.

When the Production Code was amended in 1956 (see Chapter Five), miscegenation became an exploitable theme.

UNITED ARTISTS
The Well: Discovery that a missing black girl had fallen into a well came too late to avert a race riot in a film despised by leftists, exhibitors, reviewers, and the general audience alike.

Darryl F. Zanuck, who had good luck with *Pinky* and bad luck with *No Way Out,* chose the subject for his first independent production after leaving his post as production chief at Fox. *Island in the Sun* (1957) engendered more controversy than the torpidly melodramatic film deserved. Zanuck refused to cut a special "Southern edition" downplaying the interracial antics between Joan Fontaine and Harry Belafonte. To the expected southern boycotts were added northern phone campaigns and a mysterious chain letter out of Minneapolis warning that the film would produce a new teen-age fad—"Negro-white dating and petting parties." Joan Fontaine received so much hate mail for her part as a white woman on the make for Harry Belafonte that she was escorted by police to the premiere at Hollywood's Chinese Theatre.

All this turmoil was nonetheless good box office by the late fifties. *Island in the Sun* was one of the top twenty hits of the year, although Belafonte was on record with the comment that it was "a terrible picture based on a terrible best-selling book." Introduced in the obscure *Bright Road* (1953), Belafonte, together with Poitier, became a kind of idealized black—handsome, aloof, with great physical skill and courage, and a cool sexual transcendence acceptably muting an otherwise dangerous virility. In films like *The Defiant Ones, Odds Against Tomorrow* (1959), and *The World, the Flesh and the Devil* (1959) they were near-abstractions—symbolic pawns in thrillers reshaped in the form of liberal allegories.

If the detective story could reach the stylized extreme of *Kiss Me Deadly* and the heist picture the symbolic extension of *Odds Against Tomorrow* (without breaking the essential mold), then the purity of such an ancient and honorably uncomplicated form as the Western was also endangered. Robert Warshow said as much in his brilliant piece "The Westerner," published a year before his untimely death in 1955. He saw the classicism of the genre threatened by such films as *High Noon* (1952) and *Shane* (1953), the former in its undercurrent of social consciousness, the latter in its prettifying estheticism. In the Western, Warshow thought, "the spectator derives his pleasure from the appreciation of minor variations within the working out of a pre-established order. One does not want much novelty." But on this point he sounded perilously close to the old departed audience which found in television-watching the unchanging ritual Warshow demanded from the Western.

Along with the detective story the Western provided the most stable set of widely shared conventions in the movies. Themes that alienated a mass audience in a self-consciously *serious* movie were acceptable if discreetly employed within the familiar atmosphere of the Western or the thriller. *Odds Against Tomorrow* was a treatise on racism, but it was also a heist movie—just like *The Asphalt Jungle* or *The Killing*.

In the Western the treatment of the Indian was intrinsic to the form, but the racial overtones of the interrelation between whites and Indians could easily be introduced with little thematic smuggling.

In *Broken Arrow* (1950), with Jeff Chandler as Cochise, the Indian began to come into his own as a complex historical figure replacing the simplistic Injuns endlessly whooping it up in circles around the embattled wagon train. Parallels between the Indian and the Negro were obvious in *Devil's Doorway* (1950) and *Reprisal!* (1956), both of which turned on the difficulty of Indians buying land in white communities. And miscegenation played a key part in such films as *Run of the Arrow* (1957), *Trooper Hook* (1957), and *The Unforgiven* (1960).

Because we all grew up on cowboys-and-Indians, the demythologizing of our Saturday afternoons carried a special kick in the fifties. Gregory Peck in Henry King's *The Gunfighter* (1950) was a tired, bedraggled man of near tragic proportions, a worn-out failure waiting indoors to be gunned down by a younger version of himself. And when John Ireland, as Robert Ford, gunned down Jesse James in Samuel Fuller's *I Shot Jesse James* (1949), he learned that people take the loss of their romantic heroes with unsuspected rancor. Ireland first loses most of the promised reward and then his girl, finally drifting around the country as a freak attraction in a traveling show in which he re-enacts his murder of James for an audience that hates him.

The ambiguities of Western mythology were the subject of one of the decade's most important directorial debuts— Arthur Penn's *The Left-Handed Gun* (1958). Paul Newman played Billy the Kid in a manner as deeply sympathetic as it was obscurely neurotic. Billy is essentially an avenging wanderer, his ethical impulses a form of personal anarchy as dangerous to the community as they are romantic to some of its citizens. After shooting up a wedding, the illiterate

Billy rests in jail thumbing books written in the East which describe him as "a figure of glory," while children gather outside his cell because "they've never seen anyone famous." At last rejected even by the Mexican family which has stuck by him, Billy commits suicide by wheeling on the sheriff, an old friend, armed with nothing more than an empty holster. The obscenity of romantically distorted history is conveyed throughout by Hurd Hatfield as a foppish gadfly who sobs in rage that Billy isn't like the books, and then retches into his handkerchief when he witnesses his pointless death.

French critic André Bazin called the new adult Westerns —superwesterns. "The superwestern," he wrote, "is a western that would be ashamed to be just itself, and looks for some additional interest to justify its existence—an aesthetic, sociological, moral, psychological, political, or erotic interest, in short some quality extrinsic to the genre and which is supposed to enrich it." Like the detective story, the gangster film, and the thriller, the Western retained its durability in the fifties by shedding its more innocent past, and then turning, as in *I Shot Jesse James*, *The Gunfighter*, or *The Left-Handed Gun,* to comment on it.

Even a slow-witted child, his teeth glued together with Milk Duds, was bound to remember the key scene in *One Minute to Zero* (1952). Robert Mitchum, as a military advisor to South Korea in early 1950, orders a column of civilians infiltrated with Communist guerrillas liquidated by shelling. It was one of the shocker scenes of American film, remembered years later by people who could no longer recall the name of the picture. All those gooks wasted in deadly blossoms of mortar fire—latent American racism's most unadulterated moment of expression. Even the military shuddered at the implications. The Army requested that

RKO delete the scene, but Howard Hughes knew his rights and refused, accepting a ban from all military theaters as a result.

The Korean War was America's first experience in a post-atomic confrontation with limited military objectives. Within six months of our intervention in the summer of 1950 three topical films appeared—*Korea Patrol* (1951), *A Yank in Korea* (1951), and *Steel Helmet* (1951). The note of frustration sounded early and continued late. Gene Evans, in *Helmet*, expressed the grassroots understanding of the conflict when he asked a Korean POW, "Where are the rest of you Russians?" The POW's answer, "I'm not a Russian. I'm a North Korean Communist," fell on deaf ears. William Tallman, in *One Minute to Zero,* sensed the larger symbolic issues, too. He explained U.S. presence in Korea by saying, "No one's fired on my wife and kids . . . not yet." But it was clearly Korea first, Long Beach next. The battle for *Pork Chop Hill* (1959) was significant only because the terrain itself had no military importance, thus representing a test of pure irrational determination—an early line introduction to the *Catch-22* sensibility of the sixties.

The United Nations as an instrument both permitting and restraining American combat strategy was also a new experience disturbing to an older sense of simplistic resolve. John Hodiak in *Dragonfly Squadron* (1954) wants to know, "Why don't we either get in this jamboree or out?" And Mitchum, in *Zero*, complains, "All those UN characters do is yak, yak!" Efforts to intone the patriotic spirit of an earlier war reached an absurd incoherence in MGM's sentimental paste job, *It's a Big Country* (1951). Keefe Brasselle, as a returning Korean vet, pays a call on Marjorie Main to read her the last letter from her dead son. The dead GI turns out to be quite a philosopher. At home, according to his letter, Korea was just a name. But when he got there he discovered that war, well, war makes for brotherhood. The way he figures it his mom and the football coach know what war is truly about.

When Truman recalled General MacArthur for insubordination in 1951, the entire country could understand, even if MGM could not, that the proper conduct of the complex war had reached conflicting levels of opinion in very high places. Not surprisingly there was confusion in the lower ranks as well. According to psychoanalyst Joost A. M. Meerloo (*The Rape of the Mind*), nearly 70 percent of the men held captive in North Korea "communicated with the enemy in a way not permitted by military rules." Defection and brainwashing were unsettling topics for cocktail party conversation—menticide a concept of criminality more appropriately the domain of psychiatrists than courts of law.

The salient point of *Twelve O'Clock High* (1949) was the enormous personal cost—in this case Gregory Peck's breakdown—exacted by military heroics, a more subtle, humanized image of individuals in war than Veronica Lake blowing up her blouse in the forties. In films dealing with the collaboration of prisoners in the Korean War the focus naturally shifted to the psychological ramifications of brainwashing—most notably in Arnold Laven's *The Rack* (1956) and Karl Malden's *Time Limit* (1957).

The Rack, from a teleplay by Rod Serling, takes the traditional position on heroic obligations familiar in the John Wayne syndrome. Paul Newman, under court-martial for aiding the enemy, was kept in a dark hole, questioned frequently in the middle of the night to disorient him, and allowed to squat in his own shit. But Lee Marvin, also a Korean captive, was used as a human ashtray and he didn't break. Something in Newman's character is defective—and, in an unconvincing irony, it is shown to be a deprived emotional condition resulting from an affectionless relationship with his military father, Walter Pidgeon. Just the American

UNITED ARTISTS
Attack!: The Army answered Robert Aldrich's slap in the face by banning this picture from military theaters.

family failing us again. Newman, at movie's end, summarizes himself as a man who sold himself short and lost his "moment of magnificence" by making a wrong choice.

The rejoinder to Newman's self-castigation appeared the next year in *Time Limit*—one of the few topical films in Hollywood history to reflect directly the anguish of unresolvable conflicts of conscience. Richard Basehart is also on trial for collaboration. As a civilian college teacher he is an immediately vulnerable figure attacked as a probable Communist by a McCarthyite general. Watching fellow prisoners disintegrate under pressure into brutalized animals who execute one of their own number as a suspected traitor, Basehart opts for the safety of his men against the unmeasurable abstractions of the military code. It was classic conflict between personal and state loyalties, with Basehart's choice not very different from the one Sophocles' Antigone made in burying her brother.

In the two most noted war films of the fifties—Robert

Aldrich's *Attack!* (1956) and Stanley Kubrick's *Paths of
Glory* (1957)—not war but the nature of the military
structure was the center of attention. *The Caine Mutiny*
(1954) excused irrational misconduct on the basis of
honorable past service and the need for unimpeachable
military authority. In *Attack!* the psychotic Eddie Albert is
maintained in command, although his immediate superior,
Lee Marvin, knows he's incompetent. When Albert ultimately
must be killed by one of his own officers, the other men each
pump a bullet into the dead body because they feel only by
blurring the incident can they hope for military justice. The
Army detected the cynicism in the script and denied Aldrich's
production company the customary loan of equipment, banning the picture from military installations just as it had done
One Minute to Zero.

Kubrick's *Paths of Glory*, similarly shocking in its detailing of military incompetence and the resulting cover-up,
almost never got made. Financing was refused by every studio,

UNITED ARTISTS
Paths of Glory: Kirk Douglas glowers at George Macready in
the most determinedly anti-militaristic film of the fifties. It
almost didn't get made, and the Humphrey Cobb novel on
which it was based had been around for two decades.

including United Artists, until Kubrick presented Kirk Douglas as a box-office equalizer for the downbeat story of the execution of three French soldiers for cowardice during World War I.

By the sixties a topical response from traditional patriotic perspective to American military encounters was nearly impossible. More films about Vietnam were made in the fifties before American intervention than appeared in the next decade of deepening national involvement. Not *The Green Berets* (1968) but *Dr. Strangelove* (1964) carried the shock of cultural recognition. The stock patriotism of the forties had been buried, and the demythologizing films of the fifties were evidence of a painful introspection reflected in even the most cautious of the popular arts.

5

Blue Moon, Golden Arm: The Decline of the Code

After a hard day at the censor's office, Joseph Breen once confided to colleague Jack Vizzard, "They'd put fucking in Macy's window if we'd let them." Times Square is not exactly Macy's window, but it is close enough. Already starlets gain one rung up on their inferiors by informing talk-show hosts that of course it was only simulation. Los Angeles police are always busting into warehouses to seize several thousand reels of pornographic film, only to be told by the judge to put everything back the way they found it. And yet no longer ago than 1949 W. L. Gelling, the operator of the Paramount theater in Marshall, Texas, spent the night in jail for playing a film banned by the city council—Fox's *Pinky*. And only four years later the minions of decency descended on a theater owner in Jersey City, arresting him for exhibiting the "obscene, indecent, and immoral" film *The Moon Is Blue* (1953).

After deliberating four hours, the members of the Motion Picture Association of America (MPAA) upheld the Breen Office's decision to refuse the film a Production Code Seal of Approval. The basis of the decision was that William Holden poked fun at the coy sexual antics of Maggie McNamara, whom he called a "professional virgin." The issue was less a matter of reproving an innocuous sex comedy than a question of power politics within the changing motion picture industry.

Back in 1930, using the Ten Commandments as a guide, the Production Code was drafted by Father Daniel A. Lord with the assistance of publisher Martin Quigley. Four years later to tighten authority the Production Code Administration (PCA) was created with Joseph Breen as executive censor. The PCA, sometimes called the Breen Office, was empowered to review scripts and films, suggesting necessary changes along the way and granting a Seal of Approval to films meeting the standards of the Code. For two decades the Production Code had been maintained by a federation of power centered in the MPAA which represented the major studios and their financial interests. Now United Artists and Otto Preminger, the controversial producer-director of *The Moon Is Blue,* challenged the authority of a relatively few men to determine acceptable motion picture content for the entire industry.

The original purpose of the Code was to protect Hollywood from a reformist temperament which continually threatened crippling national legislation. Even after the Code was created, Congressman Raymond J. Cannon drafted a bill to prohibit interstate transport to any movie in which "any of the persons taking part . . . have ever been arrested or convicted of any offense involving moral turpitude." In the late forties seven states still had censorship boards, including New York, Ohio, Massachusetts, and Pennsylvania, together constituting a substantial portion of the national market. Beyond this a patchwork of regional eccentricities existed. In 1950 when RKO distributed Roberto Rossellini's *Stromboli* with Ingrid Bergman, the censor board in Memphis found it inimical to community interests to show a film "starring a woman living in open adultery." At the same time, up in

Chicago at the RKO Grand all-night screenings were added to meet the demand.

The old-line studios were committed to the theory of family audiences and to the notion so often expressed by Eric Johnston, president of the MPAA, that the Code existed to protect them. But the family audience was a thing of the past. Independent producers like Samuel Goldwyn and distributors like United Artists and later American-International recognized the fact early. The monolithic audience of the forties to whom you simply sold a weekly seat had been replaced by pluralistic audiences to whom you sold individual pictures.

But the rigorous philosophy of the Code, contained in the seldom read sociological appendices supporting the individual edicts, was firmly rooted in the attitude that "correct entertainment raises the whole standard of a nation." The latitude extended to film was agreed to be less than was allowed either to literary or theatrical material, a reflection of a 1915 Supreme Court decision which ruled that movies, as mere "spectacles," were not entitled to Constitutional protection. This sense of cultural inferiority was imbedded in the Code's language: "Most arts appeal to the mature. This art [motion pictures] appeals at once to every class, mature, immature, developed, undeveloped, law abiding, criminal." In resolutely protecting the lowest common denominator among the film audience, the Code recognized important tensions between urban areas and "small communities, remote from sophistication and from the hardening process which often takes place in the ethical and moral standards of groups in large cities." In short, moral ambiguity, a central theme of much modern art in the twentieth century, was implicitly proscribed in the Code's commitment to a medium which "builds character, develops right ideals, inculcates correct principles, and all this in attractive story form."

But two decades and a World War had made much of this earlier parental protectiveness susceptible to criticism. Speaking on censorship in 1949, Samuel Goldwyn had the Code in mind when he complained of pictures which were "a lot of empty, little fairy tales that do not have much relation to . . . bringing into theaters the huge public over thirty which so consistently stays away." The Breen Office occasionally appeared rather capricious in its rulings. Howard Hawks' *I Was a Male War Bride* (1949) included a scene of Cary Grant in drag together with a string of sex jokes based on the unbelievable difficulty two people have in sleeping together when their marriage is filtered through military red tape. After spending his wedding night in a bathtub and facing a subsequent evening in separate billets, Grant dryly responds to Ann Sheridan's stoical "Get a good night's sleep" with "That's all I've *been* getting!" Such dialogue passed unscathed, while across town the blue pencil fell on the intended sex of a gorilla in the Abbott & Costello movie *Africa Screams* (1949). In a running gag a lady ape periodically chased Lou Costello with evident amorous intentions, but the Breen Office nixed this piece of business, insisting that the gender of the gorilla be changed to male. Presumably the alteration cleaned up the content of the gag, but writers along the Strip were quick to spread the word that this year gay gorillas were in with the censors.

Writers, of course, are historically experienced saboteurs of the censor's best intentions. Screenwriters, especially, were as practiced in collusion and indirection as any Victorian novelist watching over his shoulder for the imminent appearance of Mrs. Grundy. When Grace Kelly comes upon Cary Grant treading water with Brigitte Auber in *To Catch a Thief* (1955), John Michael Hayes has her say, "You looked like you were conjugating some irregular verbs." Similarly, in Lawrence Roman's script for *Slaughter on Tenth Avenue* (1957), D. A. Richard Egan responds to gangster Walter Matthau's invitation to play ball with "You can read my answer off the walls of certain public places." It was perfect movie dialogue, innocent in itself even if the laughter it produced was not. The Code, in its philosophical ramblings, seemed to allow a leniency to dialogue denied to visual content. Words, after all, are what one picture is worth a thousand of. *Dolorita in the Passion Dance* (1896) apparently was the first censored film. It didn't even have subtitles.

Often censors looked the other way if they thought risque dialogue was sufficiently ambiguous to elude the tenderest minds in the audience. In *The Big Sleep* (1946) Bogey and Lauren Bacall engage in a famous dialogue about how jockeys ride horses, but you needed to be under twelve or dense as a bale of hay not to get the point. By the fifties dialogue was even more explicit. Martha Hyer complains to William Holden in *Sabrina* (1954), "I don't want to spend the first eighteen hours of my honeymoon in a plane . . . sitting up!" And when an available co-ed in *Five Against the House* (1955) tells restless Brian Keith what he needs is a nice girl, he replies, "Child, what I need has nothing to do with a *nice* girl."

Even family pictures were permitted some adult bluing, if the business was cleverly slanted above Junior's head. Maureen O'Hara is improbably disguised as a boy in *At Sword's Point* (1952), a subterfuge which leads to a protracted sex joke involving the sharing of the last remaining bed at an inn with fellow musketeers Cornel Wilde and Alan Hale Jr. as they lustily sing their old motto, "All for one and one for all!" But probably the top surprise of the decade was a piece of shtick concocted for Jerry Lewis in *The Geisha Boy* (1958) by that old master of the double entendre, Frank Tashlin. Suzanne Pleshette innocently asks Lewis, "What is the big difference between American girls and Oriental girls?" The answer is a superb wordless gawk as the old Army joke spins through Lewis' brain while politely bypassing his mouth by a few thousand twitchy neurons.

The liberality of the Breen Office wasn't always welcome in the land. When James Cagney told Virginia Mayo, "You'd look good in a shower curtain" in *White Heat* (1949), a lady censor in Ohio ordered the offending compliment snipped. And just beyond that lady in Ohio was the Board of Regents in New York, the notorious bluenoses of Chicago, the racially sensitive theater circuits of the South, and, over all, the most powerful pressure group in the country, the Catholic Legion of Decency, whose Condemned Rating was believed the death knell at the box office even for pictures bearing the Production Seal.

Otto Preminger agreed it would have been easy to edit *The Moon Is Blue* to the satisfaction of the Breen Office. It wasn't a question of art. Preminger had no pretensions that he was dealing with a masterpiece whose perfect integrity was a deep matter of artistic conscience. He simply wanted to present to a motion picture audience essentially the same play which theatergoers had enjoyed for over two years on Broadway. But the Code specifically stated that "everything possible in a play is not possible in a film," especially jokes about seduction.

Friends tried to dissuade Preminger from clashing head on with the Breen Office. "I guarantee you won't show it in more than five theaters," a member of the MPAA warned the director. "We'll see," was the answer. Times were changing. Columbia was filming James Jones' *From Here to Eternity*, the rawest of the popular novels to come out of World War II. In 1951, when the book appeared, it was widely regarded as impossible to film. But Harry Cohn told writer Daniel Taradash, "We're going to get away with everything we can." United Artists was committed to distribute adult pictures, its executives noting with great relish that the Supreme Court in overruling New York's censorship of Rossellini's *The Miracle* —part of a trilogy known as *Ways of Love* (1951)—had countermanded its own previous exclusion of motion pictures from the protection of the First Amendment. Movies were entitled to the same freedoms as novels and plays, an idea that was a potential stick of dynamite under the obsolete attitudes embodied in the Code.

The Moon Is Blue was clearly protected under the *Miracle* decision, but what about the box office? By the fall of 1953 the exhibitor backlash against 3-D already was evident. Many theater owners felt exploited by the high cost of converting to a precarious novelty and further insulted by the dismal pictures the studios rushed out to capitalize on the fad. Both producers and exhibitors had noticed the increasing success of foreign films intended for adult audiences. Joseph Burstyn, the distributor of Vittorio De Sica's *The Bicycle Thief*, had applied for a Seal but refused to make the two cuts necessary to receive one. Nonetheless, the film played many theaters where no picture without a Seal had previously appeared.

Even conservative Universal was doing well distributing the British comedies of Alec Guinness. And rumbles were around of a new Italian delight with the unpronounceable name of Gina Lollobrigida. Not a few of her fans went to see her films and never bothered to read a subtitle. In *Holiday* Al Hine confessed his admiration for Silvana Mangano in the well-soaked work clothes she wore in *Bitter Rice* (1950). His enthusiasm was sufficiently shared for the picture to jump the art circuit and roll up an impressive million-dollar gross in the broader market. Public sophistication about at least some of the attributes of foreign films was pretty well summarized in a Groucho Marx gag in *Love Happy*. Frisking Ilona Massey after a wild rooftop chase, Groucho seems about to bestow a pinch on a risky part of her anatomy when he turns to the camera and in smiling retreat proclaims, "If this were a French movie, I could do it!"

When the MPAA upheld Breen's decision to deny *The Moon Is Blue* a Seal, United Artists deliberated briefly and then decided to go it alone, although they soon had a Condemned Rating from the Legion to worry about as well. Feelings in Hollywood ran hot over the issue. Rumors gave the

Code less than a year of life. Eric Johnston countered them with a report that every studio head whom he had contacted wanted the Code maintained. Angry MPAA members contemptuously remarked that, of course, some theater owners would show anything, Seal or not. Writer-director Clarence Greene more cheerfully predicted, "There'll always be an England, there'll always be a Code." Meanwhile, *Film Daily* favorably reviewed the *Moon* movie, stating that it was "never once in questionable taste."

Arbiters of public morality scurried to their posts as if their precincts had been invaded by medieval plague. As noted, Jersey City ordered the arrest of theater manager Arthur Manfredonia. Maryland banned *Moon*. But the Dallas *Morning News* found the film's plot "as pure as Goldilocks." When the Milwaukee Motion Picture Commission banned it, motorists braved a steady drizzle to get to drive-ins playing the film to capacity audiences outside the jurisdiction. By the end of the year, United Artists announced in a full-page ad in trade journals that *The Moon Is Blue* had returned a staggering $8.5 million in its first twenty-one weeks in release. While the figure tumbled closer to half that in later reports, the myth of massive economic disaster for pictures distributed without a Seal exploded in the film's triumphant run through between eight and nine thousand bookings. In a private letter to Eric Johnston, Samuel Goldwyn spelled out the obvious implications for the industry: "The world and motion picture making have progressed much further in these years than . . . the Code."

By the next year it looked as if the Code might survive without further trauma after all. The highly respected Geoffrey Shurlock replaced the retiring Joseph Breen as administrator of the PCA. As early as 1951 he had recognized the changing nature of the medium. Of his part in securing a Seal for Elia Kazan's *A Streetcar Named Desire* (1951) he later said, "For the first time we were confronted with a picture obviously not family entertainment." United Artists joined the MPAA in September, reducing fears of more public displays of dirty linen. While Production Code censors were routinely excising mild profanities from the war film *Cease Fire* (1954), RKO announced its intention to release *The French Line* (1954) without a Seal. But that was only Howard Hughes well into the second decade of his continuing obsession with Jane Russell's bulwark—in 3-D, yet. Eccentric, even embarrassing, but probably no worse than the spears, whips, and boiling wax audiences already had successfully dodged.

Then in September of 1955 Otto Preminger began production of *The Man With the Golden Arm* (1955), a film dealing with a subject specifically outlawed by the Code—drug addiction. Geoffrey Shurlock said later he thought the movie should have been granted a Seal, but he was obligated to act upon the strictures of the Code until amended by the MPAA. And the MPAA had firmly announced its policy in a public relations pamphlet issued earlier in the year: ". . . The United States motion-picture industry has strongly resisted the trend to break down accepted standards. We are not at the head of this parade, nor indeed in the middle of it. We are, in fact, far behind and proud of it." The parade, however, was marching on by, leaving studio chiefs embittered and divided over the second major challenge to their authority in three years.

When Darryl F. Zanuck announced in November that Fox had paid $250,000 for the film rights of Michael Gazzo's *A Hatful of Rain*, a play also dealing with drug addicts, only the most reactionary forces in Hollywood still believed the antiquated Code was a "living document," as some of its ardent defenders claimed. Despite Eric Johnston's intervention on behalf of Preminger's film, the MPAA refused to overrule the Production Code Administration to award the picture a Seal. John O'Connor, a vice-president of Universal, where unrelenting commitment to the family concept lasted well into the decade, thought *Golden Arm* was unacceptably "sordid." Other members of the MPAA resented an earlier public statement by Preminger that he didn't really care whether or not he received a Seal since the government decree divorcing theater chains from production companies removed economic collusion against controversial films.

Ironically, the Legion of Decency wasn't nearly so offended by *Golden Arm* as vested interests in the industry appeared to be. After Preminger voluntarily deleted a thirty-seven second sequence in which Frank Sinatra prepared heroin in a spoon, the Legion, for the first time in its history, failed to Condemn a picture which had not received a Seal. The favorable ruling only cast more suspicion on the workings of the MPAA, which Preminger and other independents had long felt were primarily political. Preminger called it the "private club of the major studios." His spirited frontal assault was directed not so much at the Production Code Administration as at the MPAA. It denied representation to independents as well as to top creative directors from the studios. Its serious interest in morality, he noted, could be seen in the MPAA-approved ads in which "films are advertised by detaching the bosom and enlarging it four or five times."

While *The Man With the Golden Arm* played without exception throughout every top circuit in the country, the future of the Code was hotly debated in Hollywood. Jerry Wald, always one of its virulent champions, attacked the Preminger film on an NBC television program, "American Forum." He called it a "freak attraction," insisting that he preferred working under the "main tent" of movie production. Later in a debate before the Motion Picture Industry Council, Wald baffled the writers present by asserting that the great classics of literature all appeared to conform to the basic requirements of the Code. The besieged Eric Johnston told the press he expected no immediate changes in the Code in the "foreseeable future." But more than a few cynics, including independent producer-director Robert Aldrich, predicted imminent revisions. After all, Fox already had a quarter million invested in a dope picture. And unlike Otto Preminger, Spyros Skouras, the head of Fox, was a member of the Motion Picture Association of America.

In December of 1956, for the first time since its inception twenty-six years earlier, the Production Code was revised. The bans on drug traffic, abortion, prostitution, and kidnapping were lifted, but not those on sex perversion or venereal disease. The specific changes were less important than the spirit implied in them. They were formal recognition that the movies now intended to claim the freedom in content previously allowed to other art forms. The philosophy of the Code, rooted in the protection of the innocent at the expense of the sophisticated, was eroding under pressure from a variety of sources. Foreign revenues were approaching and would soon pass half of Hollywood's gross. In turn, foreign films, which had long earned critical praise for their maturity, were becoming both sexier and more popular with the broader American audience.

The decline of original scripts in favor of films based on popular novels inextricably tied the larger studios to the increasing permissiveness of American fiction. As the list of novels waiting to be filmed grew to include *Peyton Place*, *The Naked and the Dead*, *The Subterraneans*, presumably the collected works of John O'Hara, and even *Lolita*, Geoffrey Shurlock knew the Code, as it once had been known, could never contain the movies coming to the screen. Director Mark Robson stolidly assured the Authors Club that the Code "serves as a challenge to improve a novel" like *Peyton Place*. But John Michael Hayes, the author of the screenplay, was closer to impending reality when he told Army Archerd that since *Peyton Place* (1957) he'd been swamped with offers "to write rape scenes in good taste."

As a commodity in Hollywood "good taste" suffered more fluctuations than the soybean market. In the past, it had frequently served as a euphemistic judo chop intended to keep controversial material off the screen. Dore Schary's suggestion to parents in a 1955 issue of *Good Housekeeping* that they give their children a book to read instead of sending them to movies earmarked for adults would have been, in the heyday of Louis B. Mayer, an act of insurrection, like dropping a bomb on Judge Hardy's house in Carvel.

The Code revisions of 1956 were initially regarded as an extension of permissible subject matter, particularly in the directions already suggested by *The Moon Is Blue* and *The Man With the Golden Arm*. Visual candor was still a cautious issue, although a little more decolletage was to be expected, especially if, like Stanley Kramer in *The Pride and the Passion* (1957), you were confronted with the technical difficulty of keeping most of Sophia Loren inside her battle gear as she charged to and fro fighting the soldiers of Napoleon.

Moral attitudes toward traditional values and institutions were by far the ouchiest areas for new investigation, as Elia Kazan quickly found out with *Baby Doll* (1956). In a display of its new maturity the PCA passed the film, which was promptly Condemned by the Legion of Decency and personally attacked by Cardinal Spellman from the pulpit of St. Patrick's Cathedral. "It is not rational for the artist to present . . . immoral actions . . . without at least an oblique comment on their immorality," explained the Catholic magazine *America*, straining to find a point of equilibrium from which to attack the moral ambiguity of Kazan's film. Despite Warners public statement that it felt a Condemned Rating was now more an incentive than a detriment to good box office, *Baby Doll* was a tight squeeze to return its investment. A black sex comedy with unattractive characters set in the volatile modern South required on the part of a mass audience a sensibility still nearly a decade away.

The disappearance of what Ben Hecht called "The Law of the Virtuous Finish," in which wrongdoers were punished if not actually drawn and quartered at the end of a picture, was a gradual development. Stanley Kramer has admitted that Breen Office pressure for Brando to be punished at the end of *The Wild One* deflected the force of the film. And Kirk Douglas, wandering around after being stabbed by Jan Sterling in Billy Wilder's *Ace in the Hole* (1951), provides a ludicrous conclusion to what otherwise was one of the most uncompromised movies of the early fifties. Ida Lupino's carefully sympathetic *The Bigamist* (1953) included an obligatory concluding lecture by a judge, a favorite vehicle for asserting the conventional morality required by the Code.

In the forties adultery was frequently punishable by death, especially since, as in *Double Indemnity* (1944) and *The Postman Always Rings Twice* (1946), it was often accompanied by the impulse to murder the dispensable cuckold. By the mid-fifties the vindictive mood had somewhat subsided. After her affair with the married Rossano Brazzi, Katharine Hepburn presumably returns to schoolteaching in America with good health and few regrets. But Geoffrey Shurlock, as the new Code administrator, was quick to indicate that punishment for moral indiscretions could take the form of subtle emotional anguish. Of Fox's *The Man in the Gray Flannel Suit* (1956) Shurlock said, "I feel sure that Gregory Peck's decision to face up to his responsibilities and support his illegitimate son, and Jennifer Jones's despairing acquiescence in what is their mutual Calvary, is as memorable a portrayal of crime and punishment as we are likely to see in some time." Only two years later writer-director Philip Dunne offered his latest film, *Ten North Frederick* (1958), as an example of the relaxed conditions of the new Code. Neither Diane Varsi nor Gary Cooper was specifically punished for extracurricular sexuality, and their difficulties, according to Dunne, developed strictly out of thematic requirements of the film. By 1960 adultery without hatchet revenge was a common ingredient in such adult melodramas as *The Best of Everything* (1959), *A Summer Place* (1959), and *Strangers When We Meet* (1960).

For the sex comedies spawned by *The Moon Is Blue* the way to the new freedom was trickier, the resistance of the PCA to mere joking about premarital sex and adultery indicative of the depth of the calcified taboos it protected. Frank Tashlin's *Susan Slept Here* (1954) was more daring in its details than Preminger's film but safely followed the earlier picture's conventional line of morality. As a precocious teenager, Debbie Reynolds is allowed a casual sexual awareness absent in Shirley Temple in her somewhat similar role in *The Bachelor and the Bobby-Soxer* (1947). Playing gin to see who gets exclusive rights to the bedroom in bachelor Dick Powell's apartment, Reynolds asks knowingly, "What happens if it's a tie?" Although supposedly a sophisticated Hollywood writer, Powell is no match for this repartee. Like his predecessor, William Holden, he heads for church bells without so much as one night of Technicolor fireworks to light his way.

The most famous circumlocution of the adultery theme in fifties comedy was the script "gimmick" by which F. Hugh Herbert converted a French farce into a polished example of Hollywood good taste in *The Little Hut* (1957). Luscious Ava Gardner, saddled with a husband, Stewart Granger, who would rather "massage the condenser" in the boiler room of his yacht than tool the Gardner chassis in the stateroom, has been secretly seeing British diplomat David Niven for six years. When the trio is shipwrecked on a deserted island, Niven swears to Granger on a Bible that he has made love to his wife. Herbert's "gimmick," approved by the PCA, was for Niven, in telling his story, to keep his fingers tightly crossed behind his back, apparently indicating to everyone's satisfaction that he is only fibbing about the adultery. Exacting tribute for this incredible emasculation, Herbert managed to smuggle in a few sub rosa details for insiders, especially a

RKO

Susan Slept Here: Exclamation point ballooning from Dick Powell's head was the perfect embodiment of coy ambiguity induced by the Production Code as it held the line against the new sex candor in fifties films.

twice-repeated joke in medium shot informing us that the street number of Ava's London house is sixty-nine.

The earnestness of the PCA's refusal to condone comical acceptance of premarital sex reached a point of formalized absurdity with *Happy Anniversary* (1959). Shurlock's people found that by dwelling on David Niven's and Mitzi Gaynor's prenuptial trysting place the film encouraged unmarried dalliance. United Artists, old hands by now at exposing Hollywood's cultural lag, agreed to meet with the newly created Review Board but declared in advance it would release the picture regardless of the outcome. Finally, it was suggested that three lines of dialogue should be added in which the Niven character says, "I was wrong. I never should have taken Alice to that hotel room before we were married. What could I have been thinking of?" Voice impersonator Allen Swift ultimately dubbed the extra loop. Niven refused to be a party to the nonsense, replying instead, "Isn't it about time we had a Seal for adults?" Creative people from Kazan to Preminger frequently argued in favor of some sort of classification in the fifties. But the MPAA and the Theater Owners of America studied the age profile of the movie audience and harmoniously agreed that such an act was an unthinkable insult to the homes of America, implying that "the American family can't be trusted." Always a realist, Billy Wilder asked if there couldn't instead be a classification restricting certain films to children. "It's not that I'm worried about children seeing *Room at the Top*, but wouldn't it be wonderful if the police kept adults away from *Hercules* and *The Tingler*?"

Homosexuality and by implication the wilder shores of love were still prohibited by the revised Code. But the purchase of contemporary novels and plays automatically forced Hollywood to dilute themes acceptable to the literary public although regarded as taboo for film audiences. The process of translating candid literary properties into watered-down

screen conventions was called "licking the book," a submerged metaphor hardly concealing a strongly perceived an-
tagonism between the two forms and often between the men
who worked in them. Robert Anderson later regretted the
part he played in reducing his Broadway play *Tea and Sympathy* to the ambiguous mush that arrived on the screen.
However, Tennessee Williams condoned the elimination of
the homosexual theme from *Cat on a Hot Tin Roof* (1958),
a deletion that made Paul Newman's obsession with his dead
pal, Skipper, inexplicably strident.

For *The Strange One* (1957) producer Sam Spiegel talked
the Code authorities into reducing the two major cuts already
made by Columbia to a relatively minor change involving
several lines of dialogue and some sixty feet of film. But the
effeminate Cockroach retained his implicit homosexual quality,
and director Jack Garfein had some insidious visual fun with
a scene in which Ben Gazzara's self-elected Boswell watches
his idol brandish his military sword. The literary gadfly who
follows Billy the Kid in Arthur Penn's *The Left-Handed Gun*
was similarly effeminate and sufficiently ambiguous to be
regarded as homosexual by some critics.

In the summer of 1958 Seven Arts announced it had taken
an option on Radclyffe Hall's antique shocker *The Well of
Loneliness*, a muted novel of Lesbian love written in the late
twenties. Within a few months, Robert Aldrich was making
plans in London to film a British play with a Lesbian theme,
The Catalyst by Ronald Duncan. And Arthur Hornblow Jr.
told *Daily Variety* he had purchased rights to *The Captive*,
a French play dealing with Lesbianism closed down by New
York authorities upon its original appearance in 1926. He
hoped to produce from this property a movie "acceptable to
the Production Code." None of these projects ever reached
the screen, but the PCA was under no illusion as to what
would be pounding at its door next.

Under the administration of Geoffrey Shurlock, the Code

tried to avoid the embarrassing collision of opposing forces witnessed by the public in the *Moon Is Blue* and *Golden Arm* cases. Audiences were changing, maturing. So were movies. And so homosexuality came to the screen without the brouhaha surrounding the appearance of other previously forbidden subjects. Hardly anybody noticed the homosexual hood make a pass at Harry Belafonte in Robert Wise's thriller *Odds Against Tomorrow*. And the next year, while Columbia accepted some symbolic deletions to receive a Seal for *Suddenly, Last Summer* (1960), the most outre of Tennessee Williams' plays reached the screen with clearly implicit homosexuality to which were added hints of incest and even cannibalism. Surveying the rapidly changing trend in film content, Billy Wilder mused, "Why, the times are almost ripe for a movie about a young man who has a passionate love affair with his mother. At the end he learns that she is not his mother and he commits suicide."

By the end of the decade clear victory had been achieved for most themes, although the hobbling effect of the Code's middle-American morality was seen in the denial of a Seal to both *Room at the Top* (1959) and *Never on Sunday* (1960). Screen content obviously was related to previously achieved acceptance of the novels and plays upon which so many movies in the fifties were based. A defense of the new adult subject matter could be made with reference to the more established art forms from which films drew. The language in Preminger's *Anatomy of a Murder* was candid, but it was all there in Robert Traver's hugely successful novel. The movies were only following tendencies long established in popular fiction, and as *The Naked and the Dead* (1958) amply indicated, errors in fidelity to the original tended to fall well on the side of deferred risk.

Much slower to change was what was uniquely a quality of film: its highly charged visual content for which not even

UNITED ARTISTS
La Parisienne: BB's eroticism was healthy splash from rapidly approaching New Wave of French movies. Social implications of Bardot's image were examined in the pages of *Life,* by Simone de Beauvoir, and among less philosophical moviegoers who had never before seen anyone's bare buttocks in wide screen.

the legitimate theater provided an analogous precedent. The repression of literary content in film was overcome in the fifties. But with the visual taboos on nudity and explicit eroticism the battle was only begun. The Code was strict on nudity: "Complete nudity, in fact or silhouette, is never permitted." About sexual congress the Code language was a dead giveaway of its origin in an earlier perfervid American puritanism: "Lustful and open-mouth kissing, lustful embraces, suggestive postures and gestures are not to be shown." There was no indication anywhere in the Code that sexual kisses and embraces are ever anything but "lustful" and "suggestive."

Visual candor was so timid in the earlier fifties that Stanley Kramer devised a cartoon bridge for *The Four Poster* (1952) whenever he wanted to show Rex Harrison and Lilli Palmer in bed together. What was frequently exploited in the distribution of foreign films was their greater explicitness in erotic imagery. Audiences that would have dozed off in *La Strada* (1956) hurried on over to the art theaters to see something like *The Naked Woman* (1950), although Bosley Crowther warned them they would "not find so much as an unpeeled grape on display." Then in late 1957 the most successful foreign film to appear in the United States opened at the Paris Theatre in New York. While there was no nudity, apart from a decorously posed opening sunbathing sequence, the casual animal grace of Brigitte Bardot in *And God Created Woman* (1957) was shocking iconography in wide screen and Technicolor.

The film hit New York within weeks of the appearance of Jack Kerouac's novel *On the Road* and carried with it the suggestion of the continental equivalent of a new and restless style of life, all the more fascinating because there was, in the late fifties, so little public evidence of it out there on the Eisenhower streets. The film became a near fixture at the Paris Theatre, returning two hundred thousand dollars in its first twenty-five weeks, half the picture's entire cost! The Legion slammed it with a Condemned Rating, but every major circuit in the country spot booked it. Houses which usually held a film two or three weeks ran the picture for three or four months.

Reportedly, Columbia arranged partial financing of *Woman* for producer Raoul Levy and director Roger Vadim, but Kingsley International distributed the film in the states. Early in 1958 Columbia signed Bardot to an exclusive three-year contract. United Artists immediately paid $250,000 for distribution rights to the already completed *La Parisienne* (1958), the highest deal ever made for a foreign picture. That summer Columbia announced the first Bardot movie under its new contract would be *Paris By Night* with Frank Sinatra as co-star. Subsequently, Sinatra backed out, claiming with an unusual lack of gallantry that Bardot had been overexposed. The film was never made. And after the failure of *Babette Goes to War* (1960) Columbia abandoned BB to the uncertain fate of free-lancing with directors like Henri Clouzot and Jean-Luc Godard.

United Artists and Preminger had challenged the Code restriction on adult themes and proved a profitable audience within conventional distribution patterns existed for more controversial films. The phenomenal success of *And God Created Woman* suggested that new perimeters of visual eroticism were also acceptable within a mass audience. Through a series of graduated steps Hollywood introduced explicit eroticism with more than a hint of partial nudity. Specific scenes were "double shot," with the cooler version used for American distribution and the warmer footage only for export. The process had occurred periodically throughout the fifties, but now with intended calculation the public was made aware of this newest phase of Hollywood daring.

Army Archerd reported that starlet Ziva Rodann shot her rape scene in *Last Train from Gun Hill* (1959) nude to the waist. More famous was a sequence between Linda Cristal and John Saxon in *Cry Tough* (1959). The "foreign version" with a semi-nude Cristal found its way into the pages of *Playboy,* the predictable fate for a number of double-shot films. Actresses of the stature of Jean Simmons found themselves enrolled in the campaign to bring nudity in incremental installments to the Hollywood screen. For a scene in *Spartacus* (1960) she wore nothing but a G-string, and although she was seen only from the back, one panting columnist couldn't help adding, "But there's no doubt of the nudity."

Simulated nudity became an obligatory scene, particularly in films which had little else to recommend them. Julie Newmar headed for the water in *The Rookie*, her giant towel lagging somewhat behind her. Eve Meyer in American-International's *Operation Dames* (1959) was seen splashing in a Korean stream through some strategically arranged branches. Watching rushes of *The Bramble Bush* (1960), Angie Dickinson said, "I'd have sworn I shot the scene in the nude. I hope it passes the censors."

From the time he replaced Joseph Breen in 1954, Geoffrey Shurlock knew the PCA couldn't "change diapers" for the industry indefinitely. The Supreme Court's 1959 decision overturning New York censorship of *Lady Chatterley's Lover* (1957) continued the high court's First Amendment protection of motion pictures, including the right to advocate unpopular ideas such as the acceptability of adultery under certain circumstances. The Court's fifties rulings seemed to leave to the states only obscenity as a criterion for imposing future censorship on films. And nudity, most people suspected, was not in itself susceptible to that definition.

Like many producers and directors, Shurlock had long felt the audience was far ahead of film makers in the latitude it was prepared to allow to the screen. At any rate, responsibility for film content was passing from the Production Code censors to the individuals who financed and made movies, and, ultimately, to the plurality of audiences—young and old, urban and rural, sophisticated and naïve—to which the movies themselves were directed.

The old protectiveness toward the audience was ending. The "small communities remote from sophistication," about which the original Code concerned itself, were left to contend with the dominant urban culture of which the movies were the latest and most powerful acquisition. By 1960 William Zinsser tempted readers of *Life* with the thought that they could now see movies "that would not have been permitted even a year ago." And *Time* hinted of things to come when it reported on "double-shooting" by disclosing that American viewers of *Hell to Eternity* (1960) would not see Jeffrey Hunter unfasten Patricia Owens' brassiere or most of the wild party leading up to the scene. But maybe next year.

Not everybody cheered the new freedom. Exhibitors forced United Artists to retitle *Dope Ship,* and the film was released as *Hell Bound* (1957), although the PCA had approved the original name. Industry ridicule and Code pressure buffeted Albert Zugsmith's *Teacher Was a Sexpot* through a number of title changes, concluding in the least offensive of a mangy lot—*Sex Kittens Go to College* (1960). John Wayne spoke for a sizable number of middle Americans when he complained: "I don't like to see the Hollywood bloodstream contaminated and diseased with perversion and amoral nuances. . . . The motion picture is for the family and you just don't tell dirty jokes to the kids." But Wayne's concept of the intended audience for movies belonged to another decade. The most loyal portion of the mass audience for film now consisted of the unattached urban young, wise and hip in ways that would increasingly bring them into conflict with older middle American values as the sixties wore on. To a large extent the future of movies belonged to them.

In Zion, Illinois, Onnie Bridges, owner of the Zion Theatre, worried about the new films. Movies had come to Zion only in the fifties and already he and his wife felt the first waves of cultural shock. One day late in the decade a new Warners musical reached them, and they debated most of the afternoon on an acceptable way to advertise it. That evening fourteen of the townspeople came to the Zion Theatre to see a film the marquee listed as *Darn Yankees* (1958).

6

Midnite Follies — the Kinky Flicks

Try to be cool. You're about to pass yourself off as eighteen in order to enter the Art Theater on Main Street in downtown Los Angeles. Oversized gold stars of the sort remembered from grammar school report cards cover the nipples of the strippers in the movie *Las Vegas Nights* (194?), and another lobby poster promises that Bela Lugosi has something to do with *I Changed My Sex* (1953?). The cops walk in twos while drifters from gay bars loiter in tattoo parlors thinking of interesting slogans for obscure parts of their anatomy. Old man Smith sucks wine through a straw in a paper cup and watches browsers in his Main Street bookstore. Under the counter in brown paper bags are mimeographed booklets from Tijuana, the horny privilege of special customers. The rest get a look at the latest novels of Jack Woodford and cellophane-sealed photographs of women in gartered stockings tied to the corner posts of beds.

After the war the street was cleaned up. By the early fifties the B-girls were in low profile, the Waldorf Cellar, where Charlie Parker jammed, closed. The Burbank was down to a thin show, no production numbers, no male tenor crooning "A Pretty Girl Is Like a Melody," no Joe Yule. Up the street the Follies had one girl, peeling to scratchy records between movies. The class strippers had graduated to the Sunset Strip, Lili St. Cyr doing her bathtub number at fashionable Ciro's, while lawyer Jerry Giesler made sure the towel was large enough to cover the law.

And across from the Burbank was the Art Theater, ironically named for its policy of showing every scrap of kinky film it could get away with, the entire legacy of the post-Code sexploitation flicks, exotic products of a group of independent producers and distributors who referred to themselves as the "forty thieves." Nothing more amusingly defines the cultural seam separating us from the recent past than the Main Street scratch tradition which lasted roughly from the early thirties to the late fifties.

Dating couples watching fellatio in *Mona* (1971) or *Deep Throat* (1972) and men's clubs arriving in buses to see Sherpix's *The Stewardesses* (1971) in 3-D assume that such pictures always existed. They just never made it to twin theaters in the local shopping center before. Not true. The hard sex films of the last few years have no antecedent in the public cinema. Their shadowy ancestors along the Main Street circuit left unfulfilled erotic promises clearly on display in lobby placards, the subject of disappointed reexamination after three hours in the dark without so much as a subliminal glimpse of bare flesh.

Of the three hundred and fifty films surveyed in *Variety*'s 1971 computer survey of key markets, over seventy were sexploitation features, some of them including hard-core sex action. *The Stewardesses* took in nearly six million dollars, placing it sixth among the top ten attractions in major urban situations. Nothing remotely similar in either film content or mass exhibition existed in the fifties.

Ever since King Kong got a whiff of Fay Wray and scaled the Empire State Building with her for a purpose just sufficiently obscure to escape conscious recognition, Hollywood has proved adept at smuggling kinky stuff into otherwise straight films. Apes and dames. Monsters and maidens. Deserted islands of women abandoned by men, save one or two survivors of a nearby shipwreck. These were the tacky cheats of the fifties, the allowable mythology of the unspeakable, translated with weekly regularity out there in the pulsing darkness.

Among directors Hugo Haas was almost alone in a peculiar shadowland between soapy melodrama and obsessive quirkiness. With *Pickup* (1951) Haas began a series of pictures in which an older man—usually played by himself—was fatally attracted to a younger woman. Beverly Michaels was the title attraction of *Pickup*, but she was soon replaced by Cleo Moore, a queen of fifty-foot pinup movies who was featured in no less than six Haas pictures. At the end of the decade, Haas tackled the theme of miscegenation, tactfully confining his activities to behind-the-camera direction, but *Night of the Quarter Moon* (1959), despite glimpses of social conscience, settled mostly for a sustained view of Julie London's anatomy.

One Girl's Confession (1953) or *Bait* (1954) could be caught at the neighborhood theater, but truly kinky flicks and their irregular fans were herded into the least desirable parts of the urban center. Places where the lurid advertising was in tune with the abandoned dreams of the tranvestite bar next door and the leaking melodies from the overhead organist at Dreamland—30 Hostesses 30. Main Street in Los Angeles, Market Street in San Francisco, the mythical Forty-Second Street in New York. In New York, as in other large cities, the sexploitation films frequently moved into abandoned burlesque theaters. When Mayor La Guardia drove burlesque out of the city in 1937, the old Gaiety switched immediately to film with sexploitation pioneer J. D. Kendis' *Crusade Against Rackets* (1937) promising "the naked truth about missing girls."

Thirties Main Street films were frequently concerned with

naked truth and missing girls, but their defiance of the Code was more a matter of indifference than a renegade assault on public morality. Between the restrictions of the Code and the cranky limits of urban tolerance lay enough space for the sexploiters to cultivate their strange little gardens. But Kendis' Continental Pictures; Samuel Cummins' Jewel Productions; and the Sonneys, Louis and Dan, had no desire to bring down the local heat for a First Amendment showdown. Their particular gift was to keep a safe distance between anticipation and reality. After all, unlike the major studios, the forty thieves intended to keep their pictures in circulation not for just a few months or a year but for many years. Decades, if possible. Even by the early fifties so little sexploitation product existed that the classics of the preceding decades rumbled on with occasional re-editings and title changes.

Nonetheless, nudity was more carefully handled than sensational and bizarre subject matter. Until the later fifties New York had extremely firm laws prohibiting nudity. And for the producer of kinky flicks as much as a third of his revenues depended on New York alone. Still, there are tricks to every trade. Steamy trailers often included scenes mysteriously absent when the picture appeared the next week. Other films existed in hot and cool versions, a practice emulated in Hollywood by the mid-fifties. Double prints were especially common with the burlesque features popular in the late forties through the early fifties. In the cool version the strippers worked down to pasties or net bras and G-strings, while the hot print permitted bare breasts and perhaps a flash of buttocks as the G-string sailed into the imaginary audience. In both versions the tedious tail end of burlesque comedy puffed out the film to interminable length with hoary routines in which a straight man asked a baggy-pants comic if he had a Fairy Godmother, only to get the inevitable answer, "No, but I have an uncle we're not too sure about."

A usual pairing around 1950 was a current burlesque feature with an older sexploitation classic of the thirties or forties. The earlier films were useful in clearing the house. Only those in whom prurience had passed clear through into catatonia could withstand more than a few minutes of *Victims of Passion* (193?) or *Sinful Souls* (193?). The sound tracks of these old films popped and crackled like a Fourth of July celebration, and the prints were always dark, as if daylight were too expensive to be included in the budget. The world was dark, too, full of roadhouses in which girls staggered in their undies from upstairs rooms to announce that little Mary, the newest recruit, had been shot, and "Oh, what have we done? We've ruined her life." Appearances were always deceptive. Petting in a roadster under a moonless sky or doffing shoes in endlessly repeated games of strip poker were inevitable preludes to those beckoning back rooms. "Must I take this off, too, Bob?" "Yes, dear. You know the rules."

The rules were usually matters of disagreeable knowledge. The thumb-tripping blonde in *Wages of Sin* (1940?) discovers that the big city, contrary to her small-town expectations, is nothing but a bawdy house with stoplights. And poor June in *Escort Girl* (1941) learns that her mother is the secret operator of the nefarious Hollywood Escort Bureau, the very target of an investigation by Drake Hamilton, in the words of the shredding press book, "a fine high type boy" with whom June is "desperately in love."

Nudity played little part in these films. They survived on suggestion alone, the camera cutting furtively to the nearest ashtray at the drop of anything more than a stocking. More eroticism was evident in a Busby Berkeley musical. Only the themes invaded territory proscribed in the regular Hollywood product. *Illegal Wives* (193?) concerned a polygamous sect which carried on in an abandoned Hooverville right out of *The Grapes of Wrath*. In *Child Bride* (1937) Sonney Amusements, the most prolific of all sexploitation producers, paid a Main Street tribute to the success of the Broadway adaptation of Erskine Caldwell's *Tobacco Road.*

Dope was such a sensational subject that the same film, produced originally in the mid-thirties and variously re-edited thereafter, played throughout the fifties under the titles *Marihuana, The Pusher,* and *Narcotics Racket.* Vain efforts to update the picture by introducing modern sequences resulted in a patchwork of unrelated dope orgies in which previously unseen women appeared for a quick puff and a fast strip only to disappear never to be heard from again. Somehow the narrative element in sexploitation films never counted for much anyway.

The moral tone was always pious, social attitudes conservative, if, occasionally, at near-manic pitch. "Shall modern youth be branded with a scarlet blot by various demons of lust and desire . . . or will social justice triumph?" was the rhetorical bait on lobby posters for *Slaves of Bondage* (1938?). But every warning, at least in advertising, was only the inverted disguise of a salacious promise. The potential audience for *Narcotics Racket* was admonished that it would see how the "happy, normal laughter of physically adorable girls gives way to hysterical outbursts of dope-maddened women."

All this education was received while waiting for Little Jack Little to come on in the latest burlesque flick featuring Evelyn West and her Treasure Chest or some other stripper no longer plying her trade on the once grand Mutual Circuit. Or maybe the feature was a nudist film, a purloined document originally intended to proselyte new members for the nudist movement of the thirties. These were always very healthy films whose high points were athletic games of volley ball in which the camera pretended out of good taste that nobody of either sex had genital organs. The narration was a model of hygienic enthusiasm, with the emphatic declaration that all members of nudist camps were of extraordinary moral character, an assumption apparently validated by the fact that nobody's eyes ever traveled below shoulder level. "Hi, Jack, I'm on my way to the pool. Would you like a swim?" "In a minute, Doris, as soon as I finish barbecuing this hamburger for baby Alice." Nudist films always had lots of babies in them, although nobody in the picture ever indicated he remotely possessed any knowledge of their biological origin.

Even the nudist films, however noble in intention, came to foul ends in the hands of the forty thieves. By the early fifties everyone interested had seen *Elysia* (1933) and the other unretired products of a departed national fad of the Depression years. Into documentaries on the history of nudism distributors inserted a few minutes on the grass with recognizable, if currently unemployed, strippers who sunbathed without pasties, while a narrator reminded us to be interested in the healthful, invigorating rays of the sun. More ambitious producers created their own contemporary nudist camps, usually private pools populated by happy accident with pneumatic-figure models. "From the waist up coming toward you, from the waist down going away" was Russ Meyer's succinct definition of the nudist film.

A fatiguing of the product on the kinky circuit coincided with the restlessness in the mainstream industry. If challenging the Production Code sent tremors through major studio executives, the threat of police action and censorship litigation could spell overnight extinction for the sexploitation distributor. The cost of legal defense simply exceeded the potential profit available in the slender circuit of bookings available to him. Like the studios, the sexploiter had seen a sharp postwar decline in his market, although whether he could similarly attribute the loss of his audience to television and increased competition for the leisure dollar was doubtful.

From an estimated two thousand bookings available in the thirties to the kinky product, the market shrank by 1950 to a maximum of about four hundred. The fabled J. D. Kendis maintained the offices of his Continental Pictures on Hollywood Boulevard throughout the forties and into the fifties. But by the middle of the decade, he had moved to a less picturesque part of town, his staff of seven down to three, including his wife, who was listed as Secretary-Treasurer.

The old generation of sexploitation was going under, but the new one had yet to arrive. Producers Releasing Corporation (PRC), whose more exotic items—such as the Ann Corio quickies—sometimes graced the Main Street circuit, was gone. The marginal Monogram imported a tepid British film, *Mystery at the Burlesque,* in 1950, but, in general, the majors hewed to the view of a family audience. The pluralistic challenge to this concept awaited United Artists confrontation with the MPAA in 1953 over *The Moon Is Blue,* and the arrival the subsequent year of American-International as the leading producer of sexploitation films in the industry.

In the meantime Main Street flicks jerked along in pre-

FUTURITY FILMS
Harlem Follies: Stripper in-rented fur looks more sleepy than exhilarated at the prospect of performing her art on hardwood floor in front of tacky carnival bunting. Burlesque films died out early in the decade to be replaced by nudies late in the fifties.

dictable fashion. If anything, they were milder than their durable predecessors, as if the cultural exhaustion of the postwar years had invaded even this obscure reflex of the creative process. *Test Tube Babies* (1948) exploited the theme of artificial insemination, and *Street Corner* (1948) was one of several films inflexibly linking sexual promiscuity with venereal disease. The burlesque cycle was about finished. *Strip Tease Murder Case* (1950) substituted a semblance of plot for the instant *rigor mortis* of the traditional stage show. The hottest thing in *Harlem Follies* (1950) was a fire-eating stripper whose melancholy performance combined indifferently two declining arts both in the process of passing from the American scene. One of the last of the genre was *Dance Hall Racket* (1952). The cocky hood slapping the dames around turned out to be Lenny Bruce in the anonymous days when he worked Duffy's Gaiety, where hipsters trickled in to hear him put down the strip audience with, "OK boys you can unzip now. We're bringing on the girls!"

Walter Bibo and Kroger Babb were solid citizens. Both had long careers in various phases of motion picture production and distribution. German-born Walter Bibo produced Technicolor travelogues in the forties, and his Excelsior Pictures imported *The Barber of Seville* in 1947 for the operatic edification of American art audiences. Kroger Babb founded Hallmark Productions in 1945. One of his most successful pictures was *The Prince of Peace* (1951), a religious film depicting the life of Christ. His office on Sunset Boulevard included framed membership plaques from both the Rotary Club and the Elks. On the face of it, neither seemed a likely candidate for the sexploitation field. But in the fifties both became major figures, Babb proudly describing himself as America's Fearless Showman.

Neither man had been associated with the Main Street quickies. And neither wanted to be. Their aims were in terms of traditional saturation bookings, a concept as foreign as it was frightening to the candy-butcher mentality of conventional sexploiters. Pushing out to bigger theaters was dangerous, into the nabes and suburbs unthinkable. The risk of legal action had to be assumed as a part of doing business.

Walter Bibo took a professional crew with him to Florida in 1954 to film *Garden of Eden* (1954) in a real nudist camp. With him was cinematographer Boris Kaufman, winner of an Oscar for his photography for *On the Waterfront*. Unusual projects weren't new to him. As a young man in his thirties he had worked with Jean Vigo, the pride of the French avant-garde cinema. Much of the footage in *Garden of Eden* was antiseptic, but in one dreamy sequence a curvacious redhead, previously seen only clothed, cavorts through a field of tall grass, shedding garments as she gambols. The eroticism hardly could have been unintentional, and the New York and Chicago censors flew to the bait.

Bibo refused to be intimidated, and Excelsior fought the rulings in both places. New York, particularly, was important because of its obvious contribution to the potential gross. Too, New York had relatively stringent censorship edicts, and a breakthrough there had trend-setting implications for friendly reception in distribution patterns throughout the rest of the country. In 1957 the New York Court of Appeals ruled in favor of the movie, declaring that *Garden of Eden* "has been shown in 36 states and in many foreign countries. In it the nudists are shown as wholesome, happy people in family groups." In short, nudity in and of itself was not obscene. Chicago, the notorious bluenose among major cities, followed suit three years later, the court remarking somewhat ominously, however, that the film "did not expose the private parts of adult characters." Barry Mahon, one of the new generation of sexploitation producers to arise late in the decade, subsequently remarked:

The ruling [i.e., in New York] stated that . . . when nudity represents a way of life, it can be considered showable under the statutes that govern censorship. . . . Based on that verdict, the nudie markets sprang into being. Certainly a way of life would be an artist and his model, a photographer and his model, or a nudist.

One reviewer covering Kroger Babb's *The Prince of Peace* objected to the hawking at intermission of souvenir programs. But America's Fearless Showman was never deterred by critics. He moved with the times, and like Walter Bibo he wouldn't confine his product to the scratch circuit worked with outdated timidity by the roadshow sexploiters of the past. He was one of the first distributors of Ingmar Bergman, long before the name was synonymous with the art film. *Summer with Monika* (1952) was ushered out of Los Angeles by pressure groups that found Harriet Andersson's unwed raptures too torrid despite some frames carefully darkened to save the locals an explicit view of the actress's exposed breasts.

But Kroger Babb's Hallmark Productions had its finest moment with *Mom and Dad*. Originally produced in 1944, the picture was directed by William Beaudine, a veteran who entered films with Biograph and once attempted to induce Mary Pickford to cross a wooden plank over a swamp of alligators in the twenties. She said he scared her. *Mom and Dad* was supposed to scare us all. It was one of a genre of films, no longer imaginable, that traded on our national sex nausea in the form of what were called "hygiene pictures." To a bland little drama of adolescent romance was added footage of the birth of a baby and the sort of VD films familiar to two generations of GI's. The exact combination of additional footage depended on the distributor's reading of the regional climate, although the childbirth was included from the earliest screenings.

The New York Board of Regents, which licenses all films exhibited in the state, found the birth sequence "indecent." Chicago banned the picture. Throughout the country the hysteria of outraged city councils and parents' groups was matched by sensational advertising suggesting, not entirely dishonestly, that the film the whole nation had tried to suppress was playing for the first, last, and only time in your neighborhood. Miss it and you might never see another like it again in your lifetime. In many cities showings were segregated according to sex, women in the morning, men in the evening. At New York's Central Theatre the old candy butchers were in the aisles at intermission pushing the booklet *Facts of Life,* a buck with illustrations. In Los Angeles a nurse was in attendance.

In 1956 New York relented, deciding the birth of a baby in and of itself was not obscene. In 1958 the Seventh Circuit Court of Appeals reversed the Chicago ban, pointing out that the film "combined straightforward instruction on sex with drama illustrating the necessity for sex instruction." Nobody mentioned that this dusty old article had run up an astonishing world gross of twenty million dollars by reducing sex to the level of a lesson in plumbing. Least concerned was Kroger Babb. With his drug movie, *She Shoulda Said No* (1952), the Fearless Showman departed the sexploitation field. By the end of the decade he was producing films for television.

Walter Bibo and Kroger Babb opened the territory. They proved a minority audience larger than had been supposed existed for sexploitation product. Hollywood was in the slow process of wresting a new freedom from the iron grip of the Code. Now, both within and without the industry, individual producers and distributors were pushing and testing previously accepted perimeters of taste and candor. Into this complicated maze of unexpected freedom moved a new generation of sexploitation producers, men who expected from the very first that their influence would eventually cause Hollywood to put them out of business by emulating them.

The most famous, of course, was Russ Meyer, a free-lance photographer, who produced in 1959 for twenty-four thousand dollars the biggest breakthrough picture in the history of sexploitation film—*The Immoral Mr. Teas* (1959). The early going with the film was rough. Unlike the nudist pictures, Meyer's film flashed bare flesh in all sorts of surprising contexts from a doctor's office to a beer bar. The central character, whose ineptitude resembled that of Mr. Hulot, was a sort of American Peeping Tom whose daydreams became visible from time to time.

Meyer's financial partner, Pete DeCenzie, whose PAD Productions had turned out the last of the striptease films, secured a single booking in San Francisco at a former burlesque theater. Then DeCenzie took the film to Seattle where, surprisingly, the censors objected to nothing more than a brief shot of a woman chewing on a man's ear. The nudity was no problem. They had arcade machines down on the waterfront for the sailors which would blister your eyeballs.

The parade was on. The film broke out of the Main Street circuit and played better houses throughout the country. And it played for weeks on end. Two years in San Francisco, nearly as long in Los Angeles. It even achieved critical success with favorable press ranging from daily reviews to the prestigious enthusiasm of Leslie Fiedler in *Show*. At latest count, *The Immoral Mr. Teas* has grossed in excess of two million dollars, a profit markup of better than eighty to one. For purposes of comparison, *Cleopatra* (1963) would have to pass the billion-dollar mark to produce an equivalent return on investment.

Others quickly followed in the exploding market for nudies and adult sex pictures. David Friedman, who had been distributing the old hygiene films since 1956, produced in Chicago for less than fifteen thousand dollars a nudie called *The Adventures of Lucky Pierre* (1959). It was successful, and like Walter Bibo he went to Florida to make a nudist film *Daughters of the Sun* (1960?). He remained an important influence in the sexploitation field by developing the Pussycat chain of adult theaters in the early sixties.

The former agent and manager of Errol Flynn, Barry Mahon, turned out a sexploitation documentary *White Slavery* (1958?), filmed in Tangier where he was living with friends he described as primarily "smugglers and prostitutes." With Flynn sadly gone in face and spirit, Mahon produced the great swashbuckler's last film, *Cuban Rebel Girls* (1959), providing even a small part for Bev "Woodsie" Aadland, her biggest break since her debut at six in the industrial short *The Story of Nylon*. By 1960 Mahon was one of the biggest sexploitation producers in New York, supplying the market with both nudies and films like *Juke Box Racket* (1960) and *Morals Squad* (1960), pictures only slightly rougher in content than the exploitation product from such mainstream distributors as American-International, Allied Artists, and United Artists.

On the West Coast, Meyer followed his initial success with *Eve and the Handyman* (1961) and a rash of nudies combining elements of comedy with lavishly overdeveloped and underdraped women. Continuing a trend toward socially redeeming humor, Lee Frost produced *Surftide 7* (1960?), a parody of the popular television series of similar name and one of the best mounted nudies of the period. Next he combined forces with Bob Cresse, and their Olympic International Films, together with Meyer's Eve Productions, could point to a product technically superior to most Hollywood B films of the forties.

In fact, the more astute of the sexploiters had simply reinstated the flagging B picture, reshaping it, not for the lost family audience of the forties, but for a new urban audience, restless and more than a little jaded. For an investment of between ten thousand and fifteen thousand dollars, a Mahon or a Frost could regularly expect a return of between forty thousand and fifty thousand dollars. An occasional budget, as for *Not Tonight, Henry* (1961?) with Las Vegas comedian Hank Henry, might go as high as forty thousand dollars in the hopes of a larger return between one hundred fifty thousand and three hundred thousand dollars. From the four hundred theaters comprising the Main Street circuit of the early fifties, the developing market expanded to a potential of thirteen hundred to fifteen hundred theaters willing to handle adult films if they promised little censorship harassment. In a few instances as many as four thousand bookings were achieved. By contrast, a top Hollywood A picture might expect about seventy-five hundred bookings throughout the nation's approximately 18,500 theaters.

Hollywood watched in puzzlement at the surfacing audience first for the nudies, next for the roughies, and, more recently, for porno pix of every sexual persuasion. In the late fifties the official word was that the trend was simply a passing fad, like the vogue for sleeping-car murder mysteries in the thirties. Lee Frost's prediction was more accurate: "The major studios are going to run me right out of business . . . They are going to be making the nudies of tomorrow, at least high-priced nudies . . . there's going to be a lot of flesh in those pictures."

By the end of the sixties, Russ Meyer had abandoned the sexploitation feature, leaving the field to what the nudie pioneers called "educational films," a code name for the new porno pix. An ailing Twentieth Century-Fox, impressed by his reputation for low, tight budgets and high, wide returns, called him in to do the sex spoofer *Beyond the Valley of the Dolls* (1970) and *The Seven Minutes* (1971). After being held "spellbound" by the latter, a UCLA film buff reported to fellow cinéastes that "Meyer may prove to be the Eisenstein of the seventies." It is a long ride to that ecstatic compliment from the late fifties when Meyer worked with scripts written "on the back of laundry tickets" and began the first day's shooting on *Mr. Teas* by hiring three models and renting a private lake to dunk them in.

Z
Good-Bye, Betty Grable

The philosopher Ludwig Wittgenstein was fond of movies, especially musicals. He liked to sit in the front row and let Carmen Miranda shake her bananas at him. Carmen was his favorite along with Betty Hutton. "This is like a shower bath," he whispered to Norman Malcolm, his biographer, while drenching his senses in the latest song-and-dancer from the states. Less enthusiastic was Nikita Khrushchev in his 1959 visit to the set of *Can-Can* (1960) in Hollywood. Fleshy and vulgar was his considered judgment after departure, although contemporary newsreels depicted at least the first flush of corruption in his beaming face. In a repressive culture the musical is about the limit of sensuousness in popular entertainment for millions of people. An erotic pas de deux with Fred Astaire and Cyd Charisse pressed acceptable conventions to polite limits in the fifties. But astute film critic Khrushchev wasn't fooled a bit by all those flying skirts in *Can-Can*.

Attacks on the musical aren't always from the ranks of professional puritans. I recall a television symposium in which the late Randall Jarrell greeted apoplectically the notion that the musical was, perhaps, America's most ingratiating contribution to world culture. Well, worse things have been said about us, but Jarrell's outburst was characteristic of a certain kind of intellectual distemper in the face of advancing claims for popular culture. The musical, after all, is the only genre never to be rescued from itself. Cultural fascists who thrive on converting our dross into their gold can do nothing with the musical. It won't inflate. You either like Ann Miller as a tap dancing anthropologist or you don't.

Sociologist I. C. Jarvie carried the attack to the enemy by claiming that critics who couldn't respond to the musical were "insensitive to the medium in a fundamental way." Long before psychedelic trip-outs were popular the stubborn purity of the form provided a visual education for which the eye needed no apology. Precocious movie buffs who read *Film Culture* and knew the way to the old Coronet Theater of Raymond Rohauer had already discovered in the underground films of Maya Deren and Norman McLaren a visual sensuousness which the rest of us more dimly recognized as the vital essence of the musical.

Now the musical is gone, and we miss it. The puzzle of its disappearance leaves a trail of befuddlement all the way to the top. Darryl F. Zanuck in smoked glasses explains Fox's disastrous investment in *Doctor Dolittle* (1967), *Star!* (1968), and *Hello, Dolly!* (1969) to Edwin Newman of NBC. All musicals and all flops. Zanuck's voice has a funny edge to it when he calls *Dolittle* "a catastrophe," an army of spin-off products stranded forever in dime stores. And yet kids are lining up to see Busby Berkeley revivals, applauding the man who left holes in the roof at Warners in order to show people what they had never seen before: dancing pianos, lighted violins, a geometric chorus flat on its back from sixty feet in the air. You either like Gene Kelly dancing on roller skates or you don't.

The decade's first big musical was also one of its best. Technically, *On the Town* (1949) opened one month before the forties ended, but in spirit it recaptured the driving exuberance of wartime America. It was a tumbling love song to the city at one of the last points in history when urban disarray could be passed off as the charm of high energy. For some *Blackboard Jungle* was also a musical, and its view of the city, delinquent and violent, was closer to *West Side Story* (1961) than to *On the Town*.

Universal's effort to recreate the MGM success of Leonard Bernstein's musical not only traded down in talent (Tony Curtis, Paul Gilbert, and Gene Nelson for Frank Sinatra, Jules Munshin, and Gene Kelly) but traded New York for *So This Is Paris* (1954). And Paris it was for much of the decade. From *On the Riviera* (1951) and *An American in Paris* (1951) through *Les Girls* (1957), *Funny Face* (1957), and *Gigi* (1958) a romantic image of usually expatriate Paris filled the screen. *Pal Joey* (1957) celebrated San Francisco night life and *The Pajama Game* (1957) an unlikely labor struggle in a garment factory. Most often Americana was safely distanced as in *Wabash Avenue* (1950) or *By the Light of the Silvery Moon* (1953). Topical musicals were scarce, trenchant ones rare.

On the Town was the 1949 Christmas show at the Radio City Music Hall. Most reviewers agreed that it was the nicest gift from MGM in some time, and by the fourth week the film had broken the all-time Music Hall record for a weekly gross. With its usual cultural lag Hollywood had come to the property five years after its 1944 Broadway success. While a twenty-four-hour pass in New York wasn't the poignant event it had been during the war, the infectiousness of the principals more than compensated for any losses sustained by the passing years. Sticklers who remembered the original score noted that numbers were missing in the movie version, particularly the much admired "Lonely Town" sequence. But fresh material added by Betty Comden and Adolph Green, who also wrote the original book and lyrics, was at the usual high standard they maintained throughout the fifties.

Two of the pleasant surprises of the movie were Jules

Munshin as the third sailor and Betty Garrett as the salty cabdriver with a lech for Sinatra. Packed into a congested nightclub, Sinatra complains that attempting to dance will crush them to death. "What a way to die!" is Garrett's characteristc response. Munshin teams with Ann Miller, who has been at her anthropological studies so long that she falls for him because of his resemblance to the caveman. Gene Kelly and Vera-Ellen are the romantic center, forming a dance team equaled in the decade only by Fred Astaire and Cyd Charisse.

For Sinatra it was his last successful musical until *Guys and Dolls* in 1955. He was first paired with Kelly as a shy sailor in *Anchors Aweigh* (1945) and again in *Take Me Out to the Ball Game* (1949). After *On the Town* his next musical was the transitional *Meet Danny Wilson* (1952), the first of his ring-a-ding-ding swinger roles, in which Alex Nicol says to him, "I've known you to meet the girl, bribe the family, and lock the brother in the closet on the first date."

An American in Paris (1951) helped launch the French invasion. Gene Kelly is an expatriate painter joined by Oscar Levant, who describes himself in the opening moments as "a concert pianist, which is a fancy way of saying I'm unemployed." Leslie Caron made her movie debut to become one of the last film personalities developed for the musical idiom. The concluding seventeen-minute ballet to Gershwin's music was the official high point of the picture, but a schizophrenic Levant playing all orchestral instruments while simultaneously conducting the "Concerto in F" was a cinematic tour de force. Levant's presence in the film brought a rare glimpse of jangled nerves to musical comedy. Listening to Georges Guetary and Kelly unwittingly discuss their mutual love for the same Leslie Caron, Levant twitches through a spectacular routine of neurotic oralism. Cigarettes, coffee, and brandy all seem to find their way to his mouth at the same time, culminating in the disastrous attempt to drink from a coffee cup without first removing a cigarette from between his lips. When Guetary concludes his eulogy to Caron with the assertion "You only find love once," Levant mordantly replies, "That many times?"

In the early fifties low budget musicals still arrived on nearly a weekly basis, although rising costs and television competition were threatening the healthy continuation of the genre, at least in its less grandiose instances. For many the chorus line of Ed Sullivan's "Toast of the Town" or Snooky Lanson on "Your Hit Parade" was more agreeable and less geographically distant than the latest Virginia Mayo–Dennis Morgan vehicle from Warners. By 1953 musical releases were down from the sixty-five productions of a decade earlier to a still considerable thirty-eight films. In another decade the number would drop to four, with two of these dismal flops and one a singing cartoon.

One by one, personalities who largely had been identified with the musical disappeared. Betty Grable, a top Fox attraction throughout the forties, was paired with Dan Dailey in *My Blue Heaven* (1950) and *Call Me Mister* (1951). The latter was a resurrected Broadway hit of the immediate postwar years, but in the former, a Hollywood original, Grable and Dailey were radio stars as the industry bravely entered the decade with the pretense that nobody had yet heard of television. In 1952, for the first time in ten years, Betty Grable was not among the top ten box-office stars. She made her farewell with two pictures in 1955. In *Three for the Show* she was accidentally married to both Jack Lemmon and Gower Champion, while in her last film, *How to Be Very, Very Popular*, she lost the spotlight to underrated Sheree North in a dynamite rock number.

Ubiquitous Doris Day appeared in a number of Warners attempts to recapture the nostalgic success of Vincente Minnelli's forties classic *Meet Me in St. Louis. On Moonlight Bay* (1951) and *By the Light of the Silvery Moon* celebrated family life in earlier and presumably gentler periods of our national history. In both pictures Leon Ames recreated his popular role of the American dad in *St. Louis*, with Rosemary DeCamp replacing Mary Astor as Mom, and Mary Wickes as the tart but lovable maid, a sentimental middle-class institution almost as removed from the contemporary scene as the Booth Tarkington characters on which *Moonlight Bay* was based.

After *Romance on the High Seas* (1948), Doris Day quickly became the hardest worked performer in musical pictures. Basically a singer and only indifferently a dancer, she changed partners with regularity. Gordon MacRae squired her in both *Moonlight Bay* and *Silvery Moon* as well as in *Tea for Two* (1950). She danced with Gene Nelson in *Lullaby of Broadway* (1951) and with Ray Bolger in *April in Paris* (1952). She was *Calamity Jane* (1953) to a robust Howard Keel as Wild Bill Hickok. Her image as a freshly scrubbed innocent was indestructible. In *I'll See You in My Dreams* (1952) Danny Thomas, as songwriter Gus Kahn, aged throughout the musical biography, while Doris Day, as Kahn's wife, mysteriously remained the same age despite children, two world wars, and her husband's heart attack. After her successful portrait of twenties singer Ruth Etting in *Love Me or Leave Me* (1955) and her role as a perky labor representative in *The Pajama Game*, Doris Day made the transition from musicals to dramatic parts, a rare accomplishment she shared with Janet Leigh and few other refugees from musical comedy. By the end of the decade she was drawing dividends on her early investment in middle American virtue. She was the perfect foil for sexually aggressive males of ultimately honorable intention in the cycle of comedies beginning with Ross Hunter's *Pillow Talk* (1959).

Bombastic Betty Hutton wowed them with her version of "Arthur Murray Taught Me Dancing in a Hurry" in her feature film debut in *The Fleet's In* (1942). But after appearances with Fred Astaire in *Let's Dance* (1950) and as Annie Oakley in *Annie Get Your Gun* (1950), she suddenly disappeared from musicals with a final role as Blossom Seeley in the vaudeville biography *Somebody Loves Me* (1952). By the mid-fifties the list of stars no longer around because of the decline of musicals was more depressing than a tap dancer with a broken leg.

Eddie Bracken was gone early, *About Face* (1952) the amusing incompetent's last musical. Comic dancer Donald O'Connor quietly vanished until the sixties after *The Buster Keaton Story* (1957), although his final musical was *Anything Goes* (1956) a year earlier. His forties partner, Peggy Ryan, had already bowed out with *All Ashore* (1953). Dick Haymes was in that one but was gone after *Cruisin' Down the River* later the same year. The post-Presley decline of the crooner also ended Tony Martin's movie career with *Let's Be Happy* (1957). Vera-Ellen, one of the two or three major romantic dance leads in film history, ended her twelve years in pictures in the same movie. With few regrets Kathryn Grayson left films in 1956 for the Broadway stage. Versatile Gloria DeHaven waved good-bye in *The Girl Rush* (1955), and promising Sheree North was hardly warmed up before the game was over.

Most of the musical talent carefully assembled by the studios in the forties was gone from the screen by the end of the decade. The Broadway blockbusters dominating the last years of the fifties either largely retained the original casts, as in *Li'l Abner* (1959), or featured such eccentric surprises as Marlon Brando and Jean Simmons in *Guys and Dolls*, Kim Novak in *Pal Joey*, or Tab Hunter in *Damn Yankees*.

The uniquely talented Danny Kaye was one of the few musical survivors of the forties. After *On the Riviera* he formed his own production company, maintaining control of properties suitable to his distinctive style. *Knock on Wood* (1954) and *The Court Jester* (1956) were whimsical fare in which the creaking of the basic narrative was hard to hear over Sylvia Fine's jet-speed lyrics.

A trend toward light opera quickly burned itself out in films like *The Desert Song* (1953), *Melba* (1953), *Deep in My Heart* (1954), and *The Student Prince* (1954), the last one of several pictures utilizing the voice of Mario Lanza. The cycle finally expired with *The Vagabond King* (1956), in which Kathryn Grayson starred opposite a continental singer with the unlikely name of Oreste. Cultural purists preferred Tito Gobbi in Italian anyway. Those accustomed to candelabra with their Chopin had a chance, if they moved quickly, to see television favorite Liberace in *Sincerely Yours* (1955).

The musical is a deeply centrist form, dependent for consistent popular success on widely shared sentiments no less than sizable budgets. The decline of the family as a convincingly stable institution in films occurred simultaneously with the abandonment of the Hollywood musical for the occasional Broadway smash. Conventions on the fade were on view in such marginal pictures as *Catskill Honeymoon* (1950), in which credible witnesses insisted that New Yorkers were amused by the tune "Ten Cents a Bagel." Lippert Pictures distributed the minstrel show *Yes Sir, Mr. Bones* (1951) at about the time Warners put Doris Day in blackface for a period routine in *I'll See You in My Dreams*. That same year Tony Martin warbled a chorus of "There's No Tomorrow" ("O Sole Mio") in Italian before donning a warbonnet for a campy Indian number in *Two Tickets to Broadway* (1951). One of Betty Grable's last songs vigorously asserted that "Girls like a sudden show of affection/But not so much they need a bulldog's protection." The line typified an intended raciness turning over into ho-hum for portions of the audience about to encounter Bardot, abortions, and the sexual politics of Elizabeth Taylor once MGM finally allowed her to put National Velvet out to pasture.

The kids wanted rock and the old folks wouldn't leave the tube for anything less than *Oklahoma!* (1955) or *South Pacific* (1958). These were the remembered classics of their own youth, resurrected in Todd-AO and rubbed to a fine edge of nostalgia by memories of other times and other places before a recognizable America began to vanish right before their eyes.

The best of the decade? Writing in the early sixties, John Cutts yearned for the tradition of Hollywood originals which ended in the fifties. His own favorite, *Singin' in the Rain* (1952), spoofed Hollywood in the early days of sound, with loving references to Busby Berkeley, Bobby Clark, and George Raft. Stanley Donen, who had directed *On the Town* at twenty-five, co-directed *Rain* with Gene Kelly, while the screenplay and special lyrics were by Betty Comden and Adolph Green. Donen was also responsible for *Seven Brides for Seven Brothers* (1954), highlighted by Michael Kidd's sensationally acrobatic choreography, followed by *It's Always Fair Weather* (1955), a bittersweet reprise of *On the Town* undervalued by critics who found it too caustic and less joyous than its predecessor. Cyd Charisse's boxing number and a rare film appearance by Michael Kidd were worth the recently rising price of admission.

In the second half of the decade MGM lost the prominent command of the musical which it had exercised since the early forties. Donen went to Paramount for *Funny Face* (1957), arguably the last of the great Hollywood originals, although its initial conception was as an unproduced theater piece to be called *Wedding Day*. Noted photographer Richard Avedon was consultant to Donen, and the film's visual flair from the crimson dark room of "I Love Your Funny Face" through the split screen energy of "Bonjour Paris!" to the softly filtered shots of Astaire and Hepburn dancing on the banks of a lake by a country church was unequaled in the use of atmospheric color.

MGM
The Band Wagon: Famous Charisse legs dominate poster art for one of MGM's brightest musicals.

Donen's only rival for sustained excellence was MGM's master of Americana, Vincente Minnelli, whose films won both of the two Oscars for Best Picture given to musicals in the fifties. The first was in 1951 for *An American in Paris,* the second in 1958 for *Gigi.* Less pretentious and sticky than either, however, was *The Band Wagon* (1953), in which omnipresent Comden and Green conducted a spirited put-down of highbrow affectations, with the Astaire-Charisse "Girl Hunt" ballet a surrealistic swipe at the stylized violence of Mickey Spillane.

Early in 1960, while waiting for troop shipment from Fort Dix, I ducked in out of the winter sleet along Broadway to catch Bert Stern's *Jazz on a Summer's Day* (1960). Lovely swooping helicopter shots of motorboats and house parties intercut with scenes of the Newport Jazz Festival provided choreography and music far removed from anything associated with Hermes Pan or MGM. A shoulder-packed Eclair and an instinct for an emerging culture allowed film makers like D. A. Pennebaker, Richard Leacock, and the Maysles brothers to follow Stern in creating the pop documentaries of the sixties.

The artifice of the Broadway-Hollywood musical was headed, as one critic put it, toward the "ice age." By 1971 only two of the fifty top-grossing pictures were traditional musicals. In 1972 the startling backdrop of *Cabaret* included homosexuality, anti-Semitism, and the rise of German fascism. Anyone in the fifties who had suggested such subject matter as proper for a musical immediately would have been packed off on his own private road show to Camarillo.

8
Beats, Bikers, and Rebellious Youth

Among the hot sellers of the late forties were several novels that were required reading for everyone within shouting distance of puberty. Paperbacks were rapidly converting spare corners of drugstores into juvenile information centers. They put us in touch with adult culture without the intermediate embarrassment of submitting torchy items to the inspection of librarians. For a quarter you got Mike Hammer in a Signet edition. A dime more bought you *Forever Amber*, a windy bore whose extra bulk bulged under the covers if an unexpected parent invaded without knocking.

If you were a younger teen-ager the new novels about the war were as exotically distant as Frank Yerby's pirates. All I remembered about the war was that I had inherited a sailor's cap, which I incongruously wore while listening to the Air Force song and saluting a four-color portrait of General MacArthur. An Italian family suddenly moved out of the neighborhood. And we had won.

Certain books connected with personal experience, however oblique the point of contact. For me Irving Shulman's *The Amboy Dukes* was the first such book. I responded to it in an intuitive personal way as I didn't to the obvious mayhem in Spillane. Mike

Hammer was brutal and sadistic, yet he was as artificial as the author's earlier creation, *The Human Torch*. His violence didn't seem any more real to me than the epigrammatic nonsense Charlie Chan employed to rebuke his variously numbered sons.

I quickly lost interest in Mike Hammer. After *I, the Jury* I passed him by, only returning to him years later when I was inclined, rather self-consciously, to "study" him, like Orwell scratching his head over the implications to Western civilization of the popularity of *No Orchids for Miss Blandish*. Early or late, Hammer never entered my bloodstream. Not so with the Dukes.

UNIVERSAL
City Across the River: Erotic imagery of late forties paperback reprint of *The Amboy Dukes* is too pronounced for poster art of 1949 movie based on the Irving Shulman novel. Kids in *City Across the River* would have been at home with the Bowery Boys; pair on book cover are well beyond Leo Gorcey, but won't reach the screen in large numbers until later in the fifties.

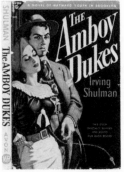

Urban high schools, however safe our parents thought
them, had a violent substructure corresponding in diminished
intensity to what I had read about in *Amboy Dukes*. The
novel was a sort of primer for what I could expect at a
Los Angeles high school of the early fifties. We had gangs,
although the Y.M.C.A. preferred to consider them clubs
under its nominal supervision. I never saw any zip guns,
but there were plenty of wrist pins, and more than a few
cars carried tire chains in the trunk. Instead of congregating
at pool halls, as the Dukes did, we met at drive-in restau-
rants, wheeling our chopped and channeled '50 Fords round
and round in repetitious displays of self-admiration. Although less common than six-packs, Country Club, or bour-
bon-and-seven, dope was on the scene, the local connection
a friend of Bobby Driscoll and so hip he wore a black arm-
band to school the day Charlie Parker died. A girl I knew
drank two cans of beer, smoked a joint, and went into the
bathroom and giggled with three boys for thirty minutes. It
was our version of a gang bang.

In the summer of 1949, just in time to catch the vacation
swell to the box office, Universal released *City Across the
River,* while Columbia was distributing the first film from
Bogey's independent Santana Pictures, *Knock on Any Door*.
Bogart's film, directed by the brilliant Nicholas Ray, was
from the novel by Willard Motley. For Universal director
Maxwell Shane had retitled Shulman's *The Amboy Dukes*
after crossing the country to take the pulse of middle America
where he hoped *City* would do especially well.

Both films explored the postwar concern with juvenile
delinquency in the slums of major cities. During the Depression every urban area had its hobo jungles. Frequently they
were populated by the drifting young, aimlessly following
the seasons: south in summer, west to occasional harvest
work in the fall, and north in winter to where the missions

were best and there was some chance of warmth, if only in portable shelters built of corrugated boxes. After the war, with society's dislocations normalizing, the pockets of angry restlessness in urban slums were annoyingly visible. They were reminders that not everybody was cooking along toward the suburbs, two children five years apart, and season tickets to roadshow musicals from Broadway. In *City Across the River* the Dukes are incredulous when they see a suburban house with "heat from a hole in the floor" instead of from a clanking wall radiator.

Knock on Any Door was the better picture, focusing on John Derek as the bad-luck loner Nick Romano, but *City* was a truer index to the violent subculture of teen-age gangs springing up in every large city. In the mid-forties a ripple of delinquency films had appeared—*Where Are Your Children?* (1944), *I Accuse My Parents* (1944), and *Delinquent Daughters* (1944). But Gale Storm or Mary Beth Hughes, even in a speeding roadster, was a menace cut to the size of a small-town malt shop. After *Dead End* (1937) Leo Gorcey and Huntz Hall had grown older but not wiser. As the ridiculous Bowery Boys they didn't have enough gumption between them to make a pass at Ava Gardner in *Ghosts on the Loose* (1943).

The zip guns constructed in Metal Shop in *City Across the River* were clearly on a different scale. The novel's gang bang was missing in the movie, but there was plenty of tough detail, including an instructor whose solution to classroom disturbance is to ". . . drop an atom bomb on the whole slum." The accidental killing of a disliked teacher was hardly an unexpected event in the violent world of the Dukes. In off-hours they beat spic invaders of their turf with pool cues and swindle the black swing band which has just played the club's Benefit Dance.

Puffed up by our middle-class superiority, we chuckled along with Anthony Curtis at the "duded up" Crazy in his

modified zoot suit. The enrichment of our anonymous styles
by the more fanciful strut of minority groups was still in the
future. We wore tightly cuffed jeans with an intact red tag
on the back pocket the cool sign of masculine tough.

Both *City Across the River* and *Knock on Any Door* were
enclosed in the familiar context of sociological explanation.
Bogart, as John Derek's lawyer, exhorted the jury to consider the price being paid for creating environments without
hope or opportunity. They could walk the deprived streets
of any city and knock on any door to find another Nick
Romano. In *City* no less than Drew Pearson warned us that
in some undefined way we had to prevent future tragedies
of the sort just witnessed.

At any rate, both films connected in a slyly indirect way
with middle-American experience. The New York locations
in *City* looked less cheerless than presumably they were.
And Nick Romano's motto to "live fast, die young, and have
a good-looking corpse" was less a cautionary cynicism than
a romantic credo remembered long after the distant slum
imagery had faded away. We recited it as we drove to empty
lots for those chain fights which somehow always degenerated into staring sessions with everyone safely imprisoned in
lines of expensively altered cars.

Joseph H. Lewis' *Gun Crazy* (1950) was nominally a
crime thriller, but it was a more disquieting portrait of
American youth than either of the more famous films of the
year before. Not the least of its unsettling qualities was that
neither John Dall nor Peggy Cummins could be explained
away by slum sociology. They just liked guns. After a juvenile run-in young Bart explains to the judge, "Shooting's
what I'm good at. It's what I want to do when I grow up . . .
It makes me feel good inside." Hemingway explained some
of his experiences not very differently. And everybody felt
good inside watching the dancing cowboys joyfully firing
their pistols in the "I Got Rhythm" finale of *Girl Crazy*
(1943). Just part of the American scenery.

Gun Crazy was as culturally intuitive as it was chillingly
oblique, a direct ancestor to the Bonnie and Clyde cycle
and Peter Bogdanovich's *Targets* (1968). John Dall, as
Bart, was remembered from Hitchcock's *Rope* (1948),
clean-cut but blankly passive. Peggy Cummins was best
known for *Green Grass of Wyoming* (1948), and the memory of an earlier innocence lingered under the surprisingly
carnal and aggressive trick shooter in *Gun Crazy*. The brilliant scene in which Dall emerges from the carny audience
to win the prize for outshooting Cummins concludes with
the latter asking suggestively, "What do you do besides
shoot?" Dall, late blooming in all things, replies, "It's always
been enough so far."

As criminals they are decidedly attractive, with no special
tendency toward cruelty or murder. They just make a living
with guns, robbing corporate abstractions because they want
a better life than small towns and carny trailers. During a
meat-packing plant robbery, Cummins shoots an old lady
and they are suddenly on the run. They wind up in the
fields where Dall used to go hunting as a boy. He recognizes
the voices of old friends among the local militia tracking
them down. As the morning fog lifts, the friends move in.
Dazed and frightened, Cummins opens fire on the unseen
figures, and Dall, in his only act of violence, turns to shoot
her in a strangely compulsive gesture coinciding with his
own bullet-riddled death in the answering barrage from the
fog.

The unsentimental toughness of *Gun Crazy* was strikingly
out of key for a film about "problem youth" in the early
fifties. For stark contrast Monogram's *Hot Rod* (1950)
featured James Lydon, the movie Henry Aldrich of the
forties, as a good kid who just wanted to race his car on a
municipally regulated raceway instead of in the city streets.
His buddy was Gil Stratton Jr., who found rougher companions a few years later as a member of Brando's motorcycle gang. Together, they convinced Jimmy's dad to support

a bond issue for a new racetrack, a generational togetherness reminiscent of a sort of urbanized Andy Hardy.

Even films aimed at a youthful market such as *Disc Jockey* (1951) revealed musical taste rooted in the dance bands of the thirties and forties. George Shearing represented a polite version of cool bop, with Sarah Vaughan the permitted visibility for black culture. In order to save an advertising account, Michael O'Shea demonstrated the power of the DJ by making an unknown singer into a star. In a few years a variation of this exercise in capitalist manipulation would be censured as payola, but at the moment O'Shea was just an amusing example of American enterprise.

If anything disturbing to middle-class placidity was loose in the land, little evidence of it was in films. The culture in which young people moved and breathed was screwed down tighter than a drum. A college rebel in *For Men Only* (1952) refused to participate in fraternity hazing involving the killing of a puppy. He wound up dead as professor Paul Henreid exposed the latent violence masquerading as Greek fellowship. The film, directed by Henreid, was distributed by the independent Lippert Pictures. The majors preferred counting noses in the four-block lines waiting to see the latest Martin & Lewis movie. And trade papers like *Film Daily* directed the attention of exhibitors toward such monstrosities as *Captive Women* (1952), which its balmy reviewer thought just the tonic for teen-age audiences.

Until the mid-fifties restive youth were either Henry Aldrich in a fast car or slum delinquents in need of social retooling. The Bohemian young of the sort emerging in postwar fiction were nowhere to be seen. Hollywood wasn't buying novels like Chandler Brossard's *Who Walk in Darkness* or John Clellon Holmes' *Go*, although both were recognized as among the first reports on a crazy new energy polarizing on either coast. In *Go* a young writer named

Pasternak explained to the straight narrator what was going on:

You know, everyone I know is kind of furtive, kind of beat. They all go along the street like they were guilty of something, but didn't believe in guilt. I can spot them immediately! And it's happening all over the country, to everyone; a sort of revolution of the soul, I guess *you'd* call it.

Pasternak, as few people in 1952 could have known or cared, was modeled on Jack Kerouac, whose own novel about the "revolution of the soul," *On the Road*, was shuffling unsuccessfully from publisher to publisher in New York.

Edward Dmytryk's *Till the End of Time* (1946) had hinted at the new Bohemia. "I'm twenty-one and I'm dead," says Guy Madison back from the war. "I'm scrounged out of three and a half years. Somebody stole my time." His job in electronics repair doesn't interest him, and a boiling sexuality is in the air. War widow Dorothy McGuire is frankly sensual, and teen-ager Jean Porter baits Madison with everything she can get on the hook. As Madison's father admits, "Son, it's just not like old times."

While romantically inclined, McGuire is a practical woman. Her idea of heaven is not "a guy who wants to lie around the beach all day." Madison adjusts to a life whose evident emasculation he has sensed but the alternatives to which are too dim for conscious realization. Forty years at the workbench wins out over life at the beach.

Robert Mitchum as the vet with a metal plate in his skull is the sign of things to come. He's an unshaved wanderer, who casually gambles away his stake for that little ranch in the West, one of the enduring symbols in movies of the romantic independent life. His loss puts him on the road again, game for any adventure, including a fight with some American war patriots soliciting for membership in a group which excludes "Catholics, Jews, or Negroes." At the con-

clusion of *Till the End of Time* we know what happens to
Madison. He's tamed by McGuire's sensible middle-class
maturity. But we don't know what happens to Mitchum.
And we won't learn until Brando rides into town with the
Black Rebels eight years later.

Younger film buffs are frequently surprised to learn that
The Wild One was not a smash hit in its initial run. Preview audiences were bewildered, which in turn unsettled
the distributor, Columbia. Among circuit buyers only one in
seventy thought the picture's financial outlook rated a top
recommendation. Columbia fidgeted over a title, alternating
between *The Cyclist Raiders* and *Hot Blood* before deciding
on neither. When *The Wild One* was finally released, Columbia breathed a sigh of relief. The film had a Seal, and
the realistically scruffy extras imported from bike gangs in
Northern California were off the payroll. In New York the
picture was thrown away at the Palace to clear the house
after eight acts of vaudeville.

Frank Rooney's 1951 *Harper's* story, "Cyclists' Raid,"
was based on a real incident which had occurred four years
earlier in Hollister, California, on the Fourth of July. Stanley
Kramer purchased the piece and assigned screenwriter Ben
Maddow to the project. Maddow proved unemployably involved with the HUAC, and he was replaced by John Paxton, author of such respected screenplays as *Murder, My
Sweet* (1945), *Cornered* (1945), and *Crossfire* (1947).

Working with Kramer, Paxton completely refocused the
original story, reducing the violence and creating a morally
ambiguous atmosphere to replace the simplistic confrontation
between brutal bikers and good townspeople. The censors
didn't like it. The script seemed to suggest that there was a
latent fascism in middle America even more horrific than
the hipster nihilism of the Black Rebels. The wrangling
continued up to a few weeks before production, with the
concluding "lecture" to Brando by fatherly state trooper

Jay C. Flippen part of the compromise exacted by the PCA.

Despite the squash of fifties censorship, *The Wild One* was the first film clash between straight and hipster America. It was one of the few pictures to pose a style of life, however inarticulate, directly in conflict with middle-American values without copping out into a sociological explanation of misfits and what to do about them. Critical reaction to the movie was hostile. *Time* dismissed it. Liberal critics, refusing to see the picture before them, anchored their grumbling in adjustment psychology. Gerald Weales, in an article on the "apotheosis of the immature" in *The Reporter*, wrote that "his [Brando's] orientation with the cyclists and against the town was part of the adolescent protest against a society in which it cannot yet take part."

But who wanted to take part in a "society" of cowardly cops, avaricious businessmen, gray mumblers without conviction, and sadistic bullies willing to use "one end of the gun or the other"? Certainly not Mary Murphy, whose part was the most brilliant addition to Rooney's original story made by Paxton and Kramer. In the *Harper's* story Cathy is a vague character, seventeen, engaged to a local merchant. She has no contact with the bikers until one accidentally knocks her down, killing her in a bizarre scene in which the motorcyclists drive directly into the lobby of her father's hotel. In the movie Cathy is older, unattached, and obviously less than enamored by her life as a waitress in her uncle's restaurant. Yet she is hardly more articulate about her aspirations than the famously incoherent Brando.

The Brando character in "Cyclists' Raid" was named Gar Simpson and spoke with unbelievable militaristic elegance. The memorable dialogue between Brando and Mary Murphy was entirely Paxton's, a grafting of hipster slang onto the newly emerging biker mystique. Clearly attracted by an unfamiliar style, Murphy asks where the bikers are going. Brando answers, "Oh, man, we just gonna *go*!" echoing the

COLUMBIA
The Wild One: Marlon Brando "explains" the new counter culture to Mary Murphy in decade's most mythically potent film. She digs it, almost.

MGM
Blackboard Jungle: Vic Morrow re-educates teacher Glenn Ford in kind of violent movie *Time* saw in part "responsible for the repulsive picture of U.S. life" abroad.

title of John Clellon Holmes' beat novel of two years earlier. Murphy doesn't understand. Where do they go, is it like a picnic? "A picnic! Man, you are too square . . . If you're gonna be cool, you gotta wail!" Brando's effort to express an alternate consciousness of time and place is too elliptical for her. She was going to take a trip once, too, with her father, to Canada. "What happened?" Brando asks. "We didn't go," says Murphy, her voice condensing into the single experience all the other short-circuited trips in her life. "Crazy!" says Brando. End of scene. And a beautiful one it is.

Mary Murphy was about where many of us were in the fifties, in restless tension between the oppressive but respectable eight-to-fours and the chaotic but magnetic hipster culture building up secretly around us. She was a square, and at the same time a potential defector from a middle America of boozy fathers and barely suppressed greed and violence. She wanted to go, too, and beyond Canada. Examining her own confused feelings, she was reduced to a repeated litany of "It's crazy" in ironic apposition to Brando's jive talk. She stayed on, but the middle class had been invaded. Jack Kerouac, sweating out rejection slips on his version of the trip mystique, must have been amused when the sheriff, after exonerating Brando for his part in the accidental death of an old man, ordered his men to "put him on the road."

For many young people *The Wild One* was a romantic introduction to the outsider who maintains a solid code against both society and the subculture in which he travels. Brando's rescue of Mary Murphy from his own Black Rebels substituted the urban motorcycle for the Western horse, unifying in a nearly subliminal image an old tradition clearly past with a new one barely emerging. Adult contempt for the picture was answered in a sudden flourishing of leather jackets. Brando's spacey style and ambiguous sensuality proved a puzzling Rorschach to a repressed time. An Eastern critic prickled over a face "excessively sensitive, almost effeminate" and a walk that "slouches, ambles, almost minces," while members of a San Francisco bike gang, precursors of the Hell's Angels, drank wine in the balcony of a Market Street theater, and "cheered like bastards" to "see ourselves right there on the screen."

The two definitive youth-culture pictures of the decade— *Blackboard Jungle* and *Rebel Without a Cause*—appeared in 1955, both wildly successful and both deeply disturbing to the adult community. *Blackboard Jungle* was a throwback to *City Across the River*, the violence notably escalated in the intervening years. In *City* the shooting of the teacher was accidental, but Vic Morrow pulling a knife on Glenn Ford was as intentional as apple for the teacher in days gone by. Conventional respect for authority could rupture at any moment with no guarantee that disorder would be checked this side of the switchblade.

The violence bothered people. Only the year before Arthur L. Mayer had warned that the continually shrinking family audience was offended as "Hollywood's previous flirtation with sadism" hardened into a "fixation." Eisenhower's Ambassador to Italy, Clare Boothe Luce, protested the inclusion in the Venice Film Festival of *Blackboard Jungle* as an official American entry. The film was withdrawn, and MGM production chief Dore Schary declared the action "flagrant political censorship." *Time* replied that culturally distorted novels and movies "far more than Communist propaganda" were "responsible for the repulsive picture of U.S. life" in foreign countries.

Less noticed but more important than the violence in *Blackboard Jungle* was the implication of irreversible cultural tensions. Richard Kiley, in an effort to communicate with his students, brings his prized collection of swing records to class. After all, that's what the young toughs in *City Across the River* listened to only five years earlier. The new delinquents are different. For one thing the Waspish look is fading into a cross-fertilization of blacks and chicanos—people whose parents grew up on rent parties where nobody dug Benny Goodman. The new kids don't dig Kiley's music. And in what is truly the most brutal as well as the keynote scene in the movie they destroy his version of American popular culture, sailing the fragile 78's across the classroom, while the sound track blares their own competing music—rock 'n' roll.

Rock 'n' roll was the generic term given to rhythm and blues as it passed from black culture through the Rinso white of pop culture. Into the fifties r & b was largely outside the white spectrum, an earthy music shaped and supported by the black market, reviewed in urbane pop music magazines under the heading "race records." Labels like Aladdin, Chess, King, and Imperial were rarely stocked in stores catering to middle-class whites. A small network of disc jockeys in major cities—Alan Freed and Tommy Smalls in New York, Al Benson in Chicago, Symphony Syd Torin in Boston, and Hunter Hancock and Gene Norman in Los Angeles—exposed r & b singles to white audiences. In the larger national market controlled by the chief recording companies a tune like Hank Ballard's "Work With Me, Annie" was unacceptable until neutered into "Dance With Me, Henry."

Jazz had escaped upward, intellectualized by whites such as Dave Brubeck, George Shearing, and Lennie Tristano, but the hard meat of r & b was immune to the polite seduction of European culture. That was what scared mothers and fathers when "Rock Around the Clock" blasted off under the titles of *Blackboard Jungle.* The association between rock and delinquent youth was so firmly joined that not even Pat Boone in white bucks and Billy Graham smile could undo the knot.

In *Rock, Pretty Baby!* (1957) John Saxon's dad wants him to study medicine, but he prefers a career in rock music

along with Sal Mineo and Rod McKuen. Mineo's complaint
is the implicit theme of all rock movies: "The greatest social
disease of our generation . . . parents!" Nothing redeeming
could be said about Jerry Lee Lewis banging on a piano while
standing on the back of a truck tooling through the schoolyard
in *High School Confidential!* (1958). Not surprisingly, half
the kids were stoned on pot supplied by John Drew Barrymore. Little Richard was black and outrageously anarchic
in *The Girl Can't Help It* and *Don't Knock the Rock*
(1957). Only his natural camp defused a combination too
explosive for the screen in the fifties.

A stock joke in rock pictures was a scene of kids bopping
at the hop intercut with *National Geographic* footage of an
African tribal dance, an esthetic equation which probably
produced more terror than intended comic relief in adults
trapped in early lessons from Arthur Murray. John Saxon
explains to an adult male obsessed with flashing skirts and
wiggling bottoms that the kids "dance like that at all the sock

UNIVERSAL
Rock, Pretty Baby!: Rod McKuen, America's favorite poet, as seen
in earlier days as promising member of John Saxon's rock band.

hops, but nothing ever happens." Maybe. But Saxon's band doesn't get the job at summer camp anyway.

Plucked from obscure Sun Records by RCA Victor, Elvis Presley raised the sexual visibility of rock to a level intolerable to adults. It was hard to ignore a singer whose sales in 1956 accounted for one in every nine singles purchased. Of his movie debut in *Love Me Tender* (1956) one critic wrote, "He uses the guitar as a fetish, pounding his pelvis against it, a strident symbol . . . one of the little boys who know what the big boys do." Ed Sullivan took no chances on what little boys might know. On his television show he presented a Presley bisected in tight shots by a camera which eliminated from the home screen the portion of the singer's anatomy not suitable for family entertainment. The electronic mutilation only emphasized the importance of the missing anatomy in rock. To adults heavily invested in the mambo, Yma Sumac, and the comforting culutral lag of "Your Hit Parade," the new music hinted at collusions outside the mainstream of white middle-class culture.

The previous cycle of teen-age cultism in the early forties had centered on Frank Sinatra. Now in their early thirties, veterans of front-row swooning over The Voice were as lost as their elders when confronted with rock. There seemed to be no intermediate generation to connect the older tradition of the dance band from which the crooner had emerged with the more abrasive and visceral new music. Bobbysoxers of the forties had been objects of bemused adult interest, but rock 'n' rollers of the fifties were cultural renegades. Even a "soft rock" film like *The Big Beat* (1958) presented a neatly dressed young man who secretly undermines his father to prove that all music doesn't have to sound like Russ Morgan. At movie's end, the father is a reet-talking hipster trying to adjust to a cultural scene for which the Mills Brothers obviously have not prepared him.

Blackboard Jungle inextricably linked rock with juvenile

WARNERS
Rebel Without a Cause: James Dean remains favorite pop cult figure of the fifties, remembered today by young people who were not even born by the time he was already dead.

rebellion. *Rebel Without a Cause* centered that rebellion, not in vocational schools which were little more than detention centers, but squarely in the middle class. The film was a kind of popularized preview of a book Paul Goodman would write a few years later, *Growing Up Absurd*. Nothing in the adult world of *Rebel* seems worthy of emulation, and so James Dean, Natalie Wood, Sal Mineo, and the others are pushed deeper into a secret culture of their own.

Dean finds himself floundering between images of masculinity, polarized on the one side by Magoo-voiced Jim Backus klutzing around in an apron and on the other by the leather-jacket violence Corey Allen had clearly inherited from Brando's Black Rebels. The ritualistic "chicken run" in which two cars race at high speed toward the edge of a cliff had an icy purity. Manhood was tested in an act of irrational courage from which all socially approved content was eliminated. The mystique of the hot rod dominated teen culture with an intensity that events in the adult world seemed to lack. Exploitation films from *Hot Rod Girl* (1956) to *Girls Town* (1959) included variations on Dean's chicken race, even when the credibility of the participants reached the limits of aging Mel Torme, the Velvet Fog of palmier days.

A month before *Rebel* was released Dean was driving his new Porsche Spyder to the auto races at Salinas when he collided with another car on a California highway. The young actor was killed instantly. Only an hour earlier a state trooper had given him a ticket for speeding. He had just completed his most ambitious role to date, the part of Jett Rink in George Stevens' *Giant* (1956). Of his three major films only *East of Eden* (1955) had reached the public. Now, with his premature tragic death at twenty-four casting a shadow over his unreleased work, *Rebel* took on the hypnotic quality of a retroactive deathwatch. The "chickie run," which Dean survived at Corey Allen's expense, became a macabre reminder that life often imitates fiction, erasing completely the line between myth and reality.

Hardened Hollywood flacks were astounded at the grief produced by Dean's death. Nearly a year later Warners was still receiving nearly seven thousand requests a month for photographs. Many letters included change or wadded bills, advance payments or outright bribes offered in the hope of not being left out. Hysterical fans insisted that Dean was alive somewhere. In Mexico, rumors said, horribly disfigured and alone.

The tangled wreckage of Dean's Porsche was purchased by a California couple who charged the curious fifty cents a head to examine it. Magazine advertisements hawked life-size heads of Dean sculpted from material described as feeling "like real skin." Photographer Sanford Roth arrived at the scene of the accident minutes after the crash and instinctively snapped pictures, but, despite incredible offers, he never sold for publication his photographs of the body. Maila Nurmi, professionally known as Vampira, was not so reticent. In a published article she claimed to be in communication with Dean's spirit. He occasionally called her on a phone, the wires to which she had previously cut. It got so bad she had to move out of her house on Larrabee Street in Hollywood.

The trend in movies toward moody rebellious youth puzzled adults sufficiently for them to examine the Dean cult. Sam Astrachan, writing on "The New Lost Generation" for the *New Republic*, observed that "In *Rebel Without a Cause*, rebellion is made not against parents or the law, but against the universal conditions of life." The "universal conditions of life," whatever they may be, were intuited as existing in a more coherent and authoritative form in the mid-fifties than they are today. Popular culture, when it was not actually worshiping institutional submission as in *The Caine Mutiny*, was depicting the corporate extinction of personality as a feeble battle between unequal forces. In *Patterns* (1956) Van Heflin remains in his new executive job in order to fight Everett Sloane's ruthless suppression of the humanist ethic in corporate life. But only a ninny could believe he would survive any better than the superannuated Ed Begley, an ulcered boozer dying of a heart attack in the halls where he had literally worked his life away.

John Frankenheimer's muted variation on *Rebel*, *The Young Stranger* (1957) was full of unintended irony. James Daly, as the father, was so monstrously committed to a life deadened with cocktail parties and consumerism that the cheerful togetherness of the ending was a little like seeing one of the pod people from *Invasion of the Body Snatchers* (1956) swoop down on poor James MacArthur. In the flux of teen culture pictures which began in 1955, many of the kids seemed to have arrived on the scene through some weird form of parthenogenesis. Their families, if they had any, were elliptically diminished to older versions of themselves— Marcia Henderson's swinger mother in *The Wayward Girl* (1957)—or transmuted into platinum aunts who stayed in bed all day like the Mamie Van Doren with whom Russ Tamblyn inexplicably lives in *High School Confidential!*

The hoodier descendants of Dean out of Brando—Corey Allen, Sal Mineo, Scott Marlowe—appeared each summer in saturation bookings. Reviewers worn down by dutifully reporting the critical distinctions among *Hot Cars* (1956), *Hot Car Girl* (1958), *Hot Rod Rumble* (1957), and *Hot Rod Gang* (1958) yearned for the more mature heroes of their own youth. Many agreed with Gerald Weales' request that "in

the meantime, why don't all you boys put down your switchblade knives and come over here and tell Daddy what's the
matter?"

Early in 1955, with exhibitors realizing that neither 3-D
nor chlorophyl popcorn had halted waning attendance,
Leonard Goldenson, the president of ABC-Paramount The-
atres, urged the industry to provide more films aimed at the
fifteen to thirty age-group. He stressed the need for new stars
"with whom young people can grow up." At the Paramount
in Brooklyn one of Alan Freed's rock 'n' roll shows had
broken the weekly record of one hundred thousand dollars
grossed in 1932 by crooner Russ Colombo. On the last day
of the engagement two thousand kids were lined up for tickets
by 8 A.M. Inside, they hooted and stomped when the movie
interrupted the rock show. *Blackboard Jungle* had been out
three weeks, but there was not yet a single film exclusively
exploiting rock.

A year before Goldenson's plea for more youth pictures,
James H. Nicholson and Samuel Z. Arkoff, with three thousand dollars between them, had decided to go into the movie
business with high schoolers on their way to drive-ins as their
intended customers. By the mid-fifties estimates placed 60
percent of the movie audience between ages twelve and
twenty-four, with nearly a quarter of all revenue derived
from the drive-in circuits. Arkoff was the legal brain, an
expert in motion picture law. Nicholson had learned about
movies at every level of involvement, from taking tickets and
threading a projector to producing and distributing films himself. He was frankly contemptuous of people who made pictures only to please their friends on "the Bel Air circuit."
"We talk to our janitor and to the vice-president of our bank,
to waitresses and news vendors, to attorneys and secretaries."
Possibly remembering his own days in blue uniforms with
gold braid, Nicholson concluded that "even ticket takers

No girl was safe
.as long as this
HEAD HUNTING THING
roamed the land!

NIGHT OF THE BLOOD BEAST

Starring
MICHAEL EMMET · ANGELA GREENE · JOHN BAER · Executive Producer ROGER CORMAN · Produced by GENE CORMAN · Directed by BERNARD L. KOWALSKI · Screenplay by MARTIN VARNO · AN AMERICAN-INTERNATIONAL PICTURE

AMERICAN-INTERNATIONAL
AIP poster iconography promised various terrific pleasures disappointingly less vivid in the movies themselves.

Beautiful maidens in a
LUSH TROPICAL PARADISE
ruled by a
HIDEOUS STONE GOD!

SHE GODS OF SHARK REEF

WIDE VISION COLOR

Starring
DON DURANT · LISA MONTELL · BILL CORD · Produced by LUDWIG H. GERBER · Directed by ROGER CORMAN · Screenplay by ROBERT HILL and VICTOR STOLOFF · AN AMERICAN-INTERNATIONAL PICTURE

have a better instinct for showmanship than the average Hollywood producer."

As the American Releasing Corporation, Nicholson and Arkoff undertook their first project, *The Fast and the Furious* (1954), on a fifty-thousand-dollar budget. The auto racing film, featuring John Ireland and Dorothy Malone, returned a cool quarter million. In 1956 a change of name to American-International Pictures coincided with stepped-up production of trendy shockers, double-bills with wildly paired titles: *Hot Rod Girl* and *Girls in Prison* (1956); *Attack of the Puppet People* (1958) and *War of the Colossal Beast* (1958); and *She Gods of Shark Reef* (1958) and *Night of the Blood Beast* (1958). Once a hot cycle was spotted AIP continued to exploit it to the break-even point before dumping it for a new trend. Bookings were even delayed if AIP thought a particular location was currently saturated with similar product.

Despite the promising iconography of AIP lobby posters, the films remained within the safer precincts of the Production Code. In genres mined by AIP Nicholson reported that "American-International takes a certain pride in knowing it has been imitated more than it has imitated others." Still, in potentially controversial areas AIP usually let others go first. In early 1956 Sam Katzman's *Rock Around the Clock* produced worried reactions in exhibitors afraid their theaters either would be demolished or the targets of civic protest. Although a few circuits passed on the film, *Rock* quickly grossed four million dollars, and AIP's first rock movie *Shake, Rattle and Rock!* followed later in the year.

A tiny independent produced the exploitational *Teen-age Menace* in 1953, long before Preminger and United Artists challenged the MPAA on the drug taboo. Without a Seal the film played in forty-one states before running into a New York ban by the Board of Regents whose counsel called it "the most dangerous [film] of its kind." AIP avoided injuring the confidence of exhibitors. When the MPAA revised the Code in 1956, removing the proscription on drug themes, AIP waited a cautious year before beating Warners and MGM into the water with *The Cool and the Crazy* (1958). When the grisly horror films produced in England by Hammer were successfully distributed in the United States by Universal, AIP advertising posters reflected a trend toward the imagery of mutilation. But the decapitated head clutched between the furry fingers of an unseen monster in the lobby display for *Night of the Blood Beast* was more imaginatively extreme than anything depicted in the film itself.

The company trade letter, *American News*, reminded exhibitors that AIP was "responsible for the rebirth of the movie habit among young Americans." However, nobody wanted angry parents milling around in the lobby after the show looking for the manager. Teen culture in the AIP flicks was as remotely stylized as *Archie Comics*. Carl "Alfalfa" Switzer graduated directly from the Gas House Gang of the forties to AIP's *Motorcycle Gang* (1957) of the fifties. Eroticism, extreme clothing styles, and hipster talk readily distinguished unregenerate delinquents from good girls like Carolyn Kearney or June Kenney in their shapeless fuzzy sweaters with matching skirts and neck scarfs.

The darker, more irrational impulses of rebel youth, much less the implication of an irremediably alienated counterculture, were tactfully underplayed in the company's teen pictures, although some critics thought they saw a deeply submerged hostility in AIP's most popular cycle: the teen-age monster picture. *I Was a Teenage Werewolf* (1957) was quickly followed by *I Was a Teenage Frankenstein* (1957) and *Teenage Caveman* (1958). While sophisticates invented sickie titles like "I Was a Teenage Hydrocephalic," drive-in managers added extra personnel to unsnarl the traffic backing up into the streets long before sundown. *Teenage Werewolf* reportedly took in two million dollars in less than a year, a giant sum by AIP's hit-and-run standards. Reflecting on horror films for the *Partisan Review*, Robert Brustein wrote: "What these films seem to be saying, in their underground manner, is that . . . the adolescent feels victimized by society—turned into a monster by society." Latent trauma became manifest in Howco's *Teenage Monster* (1957) as Anne Gwynne shielded her sensitive werewolf son from the heterosexual disappointments laid on him by the local tart. And in Jerry Warren's *Teenage Zombies* (1960) a distant relative to the Spider Woman tries to add a group of young people to the collection of zombied adults she has already accumulated. The teen-age monster pictures of which AIP was the architect displaced the anxieties which surfaced openly in *Blackboard Jungle* or *Rebel Without a Cause* into the more acceptable conventions of the horror film. Henry Aldrich had discovered Kafka, even if Marx was still a decade away.

American-International's reputation in the fifties was for the masterful exploitation of inexpensive products for a limited but well-defined younger audience. The accusation of Art came later, with its Poe cycle in the sixties. Nicholson and Arkoff originally objected to making *House of Usher* (1960) on the grounds that high schoolers associated Poe with literary force-feeding. Furthermore, they had never made a horror film without a monster. Monsters were an important part of the drive-in ritual. They put everybody in the mood, so to speak. In the end AIP relented, consigning its highest budget yet to the hands of the most important moviemaker to emerge from its ranks—Roger Corman.

At twenty-eight Corman had been refused a bank loan of eighteen thousand dollars when the president told him nobody could make movies for that price. Scuffling up fifteen thousand dollars from friends, Corman produced *The Monster from the Ocean Floor* (1954), which Lippert distributed for a two-hundred-thousand-dollar return. Shortly after, he signed with AIP to produce four pictures a year, including its first film *The Fast and the Furious.* Within a few years he had a reputation second only to that of Sam Katzman at Columbia for thrifty genre pictures turned out rapidly and in tune with a live market.

With *The Day the World Ended* (1956) Corman provided Nicholson and Arkoff with their biggest success to date. Corman produced and directed on a sixty-five-thousand-dollar budget. Released early in January of 1956, the film had earned over four hundred thousand dollars by late February when *Daily Variety* saluted Corman's energy in churning out eight low-budget pictures within twelve months. It was said that he could produce a film in a phone booth for the price of a call to New York and complete shooting before his three minutes were up. Corman came close to equaling the requirements of the gag when he sizzled through *A Bucket of Blood* (1959) in five days. Legend held that he did *The Little Shop of Horrors* (1960) in only two, but Corman himself said, "Impossible. You can make a picture in five days if you're an experienced director, but not in two!"

A key transitional figure between the fifties and sixties, Corman has been accurately described as a one-man film school. He helped Curtis Harrington make the trip from the underground to commercial work by producing both *Night Tide* (1963) and *Queen of Blood* (1966). He produced *The Cry Baby Killer* (1958), which gave Jack Nicholson one of his first featured roles; loaned twenty thousand dollars to Francis Ford Coppola for *Dementia 13* (1963); and was executive producer for Peter Bogdanovich's first film *Targets* (1968). Since *Machine Gun Kelly* (1958), Corman's own work has attracted increasing attention. His Poe films have developed something of a cult, and *The Wild Angels* (1966) initiated a cycle of biker pictures directly connecting *The Wild One* to *Easy Rider* (1969).

Early in 1957 in a definitive article, "Disengagement: The Art of the Beat Generation," Kenneth Rexroth wrote, "The youngest generation is in a state of revolt so absolute that its elders cannot even recognize it. The disaffiliation, alienation, and rejection of the young has, as far as their elders are concerned, moved out of the visible spectrum altogether." Certainly, the "state of revolt" described by Rexroth was seldom seen on the screen in the fifties. The beat or hipster ethic, as well as Bohemia in general, was exploited with the recognition that neither the Production Code nor the mainstream audience would condone unrepentant attacks on middle-American values.

Only in genre pictures, where the hipster paraded in his most manic guise, could the cultural tension Rexroth wrote about find oblique expression in film. Harry Horner's *The Wild Party* (1956) was an example, but it appeared following one of Hollywood's periodic congressional scoldings on violence and disappeared without apparent historical trace. Novels of less interest read by a few thousand people survive as objects of critical attention, while movies seen by hundreds of thousands vanish entirely from cultural memory. Better known was Leslie Stevens' *Private Property* (1960) with Corey Allen and Warren Oates invading suburbia for malignant sexual purposes. Hollis Alpert wrote that the old guard in Hollywood breathed a sigh of relief when the film died away without critical acclaim. It had been exhibited without a Seal, and each success in that direction reminded entrenched interests of the rough handling Preminger had given them.

In 1957 Viking finally published Kerouac's *On the Road* to curiously mixed reviews. Gilbert Millstein compared it favorably to Hemingway's debut in the twenties. At Columbia, where Kerouac had gone to school in the forties, Mark Van Doren fervently hoped that it wasn't going to turn out to be an important book. Journalist James Wechsler confronted Kerouac in a symposium at Hunter College, and came away baffled by the writer's antic style and particularly by a poem to Harpo Marx which concluded, "Harpo, who is that lion I saw you with?" Allen Ginsberg's *Howl* was on trial in San

Francisco for the alleged obscenity of ecstatically recording a generation's wilder derelictions of American duty. The general feeling was that the whole thing would blow over as soon as *Time* stopped amusing its readers with reports of the incipient guerrilla theater of Ginsberg and his buddies, Peter Orlovsky and Gregory Corso. Diana Trilling was not so sure.

Improbably, MGM brought Kerouac's North Beach to the screen. The way was paved by Albert Zugsmith, imported from Universal to pump a little life into the studio's tepid youth pictures. Like Jungle Sam Katzman, Zugsmith claimed no losers among his twenty-six films. For *High School Confidential!* he touted Russ Tamblyn as a James Dean with a sense of humor. Periodically, he issued sinister memos to the trades that his research for *Confidential!* had turned up unspeakable teen-age vices rarely seen on the back lots at Culver City. Before the returns were in Zugsmith was on to his second flick for MGM, *The Beat Generation* (1959). Ray Danton, as a psychopathic killer, bore an odd facial resemblance to Kerouac, a coincidence probably not lost on Zugsmith, who always loved bizarre casting.

The internal pranks of Zugsmith's exploitation films are a subject all to themselves, but MGM's most fateful collision with Bohemia was *The Subterraneans* (1960). In early 1958 Tri-Way Productions took an option on Kerouac's *On The Road,* but the inability to secure financing caused the project to founder. MGM had offered fifty thousand dollars outright for *Road*, and had subsequently purchased the less well-known short novel, *The Subterraneans*. Denis and Terry Sanders, UCLA film graduates with one feature and a screenplay under their collective belts, were assigned as director and associate producer respectively.

Two weeks into production the roof blew off, and MGM summarily replaced the Sanderses with director Ranald Mac-Dougall. Compromises with Kerouac's book had begun with making the feminine lead, played by Leslie Caron, a neurotic white French girl instead of a black Reichian searching for the perfect orgasm. According to the Sanderses things got worse thereafter as producer Arthur Freed insisted to them, "I don't care if she's been with forty men—the girl is a virgin." Freed denied the remark as well as the accusation that MGM was foisting a Victorian morality onto a story about amoral hipsters in San Francisco's North Beach. Nonetheless, in MGM's Bohemia beat writer George Peppard is forced to complain, "I'm twenty-eight, and I'm still looking for someone to talk to." His mother, with whom he lives, suggests they listen to a recording of "The Blue Danube" instead. It wasn't much to build a revolution on, even in the fifties.

By the end of the decade every studio was producing films which intentionally or not implied that only young people had style and intelligence in a world where adults were characteristically drunk, dense, or vicious. Eric Johnston warned studio chiefs that the Code would tighten up on films which repeatedly exploited the violent subculture of teen-agers. Few believed his comments were other than window dressing designed to appease the more conservative critics of the industry. A study financed by the MPAA in 1958 indicated that the decade's drift toward a more youthful audience bunched in the teens through early twenties had reached the point where 72 percent of all moviegoers were under thirty. The MPAA's own Children's Film Library had fallen into disuse. Except for Disney, the studios ignored the audience under twelve.

At a luncheon for exhibitors in Miami Beach the lime sherbet hardly had a chance to melt before Jerry Wald unexpectedly rose to attack his hosts, American-International. Reciting a string of AIP's recent titles to which various parents' groups had objected, he urged the company to "lift its horizons." James Nicholson waited patiently for Wald to finish, and then replied that he would rather send his own children to an AIP horror film than to, say, *God's Little Acre*

(1958). "Our monsters don't drink, smoke, or lust," he said. Every AIP film had received a Seal and none had ever been Condemned by the Legion of Decency. There was less suggestiveness in them than in Wald's own *Peyton Place* or *No Down Payment* (1957). Then, with exhibitors hunched over crumpled napkins and cold cups of coffee, unexpected witnesses to the sort of internecine feud they usually only read about, Nicholson quietly reminded Wald who had paid for his lunch, and noted that AIP's schedule for the coming year was the most ambitious in its uniquely profitable career.

Look! Mara Corday's in the street in her nightgown. And there's no telling where Leo G. Carroll's giant tarantula is. Only a moment ago it was at Mara's window, a hairy insect voyeur peeping as she undressed for bed. Carroll's fascination with forced giantism once again prove the dangerous consequences of experimental science. In *Tarantula* (1955) John Agar saves us, as he does so often in the decade, this time bringing in the Air Force to bomb the huge creature as it wobbles across the horizon terrorizing everything in its path.

Throughout the fifties our repressed paranoia visited us reshaped in the basic mythology of science fiction. The popular mutation size cycle of the mid-fifties was perfect embodiment of what historian Richard Hofstadter called the "paranoid style." Not the Communists, or Wall Street, or the beatniks were responsible for the decline and fall of it all. Instead we had giant scorpions, claw monsters, spiders, ants, interstellar pituitary cases, even a fifty-foot woman, although admittedly she was less interested in social havoc than in the wandering attentions of her midget husband. According to Hofstadter, in the "paranoid style" history is viewed as a vast conspiracy "set in motion by demonic forces of almost transcendent

My God! It's a 50-Foot Woman!

power." The stakes are nothing less than "the birth and death of whole worlds." Each Saturday night we witnessed the latest hostile surprise created by an environment more capriciously malignant than anything McCarthy promised in his most lunatic moments.

Most of the giant mutations roaming the fifties were created by atomic radiation. Intellectuals could puzzle over the implications of the nuclear age with Gunther Anders in his 1956 *Dissent* article in which he called for a rebirth of moral imagination in a Faustian era. The rest of us got the news from scientist Edmund Gwenn in *Them!* (1954). Twelve-foot ants, the product of atomic testing in New Mexico, were loose in the West. They wrecked freight cars, devoured forty tons of sugar, and wandered into the sewers of Los Angeles to hatch millions of young. Fortunately, the military located the major nest in Drain #267 and liquidated the pregnant females with grenades and flame throwers. The paranoid note was sounded in Gwenn's concluding observation that man had entered the atomic era without knowing what to expect.

Radiation also launched the *Attack of the Crab Monsters* (1957) and produced the insect army employed by the bug-eyed invaders from Astron Delta in *Killers from Space* (1954). Underwater testing awakened from his prehistoric slumber *The Beast From 20,000 Fathoms* (1953), the first in a series of monsters from the deep. Giant grasshoppers threatened Chicago in *Beginning of the End* (1957). And Army officer Glenn Langan grew as irritable as he was enormous after exposure to radiation in *The Amazing Colossal Man* (1957). With mutants stalking every point of the globe it was no wonder Sonny Tufts wanted to use his life savings to convert a cave into a bomb shelter in *Run For the Hills* (1953).

The most poignant of these disastrous dislocations in size occurred in Jack Arnold's *The Incredible Shrinking Man*

UNIVERSAL
The Incredible Shrinking Man: Even on a storage shelf in his cellar, Grant Williams finds no escape from hostile environment in one of the best of the paranoid cycle of science fiction films.

(1957). Subjected to a strange radioactive cloud while sunbathing on the deck of a boat in the middle of the ocean, Grant Williams slowly begins to diminish in size. At first the changes are subtle. His clothes are baggy. His wife kids him about losing weight. Soon the shrinkage passes the joking stage. A doctor confesses that the case is unique, possibly hopeless. Williams' wife promises to stick with him as long as he wears the wedding band symbolizing their union. As Williams turns the ignition key to start the car the ring slides from his finger to the floor.

In other mutation flicks stable institutions restore order, but there's no help for the shrinking man. An affair with a midget ends when he becomes too small for her. He cowers in the corner of a giant chair while his wife explains to reporters that he can't see them. Gradually his ability to cope with a normal environment declines until he lives in a specially constructed doll house, and worries that his wife will forget to lock up the cat when she goes shopping.

For seven hundred thousand dollars Universal-International designed twenty-one-foot pencils and a four-hundred-pound scissors, outsize furniture, and a mountainous papier-mâché cheese. These were components of a world grown so hostile that a man can drown in his own cellar and has to fight a tarantula with a sewing needle to get a decent meal. *Shrinking Man* was a metaphorical vision of paranoia not blunted even by the pseudoreligious ending in which Williams concludes that "to God there is no zero," as he escapes from his cellar through pores in a screen.

Within months of Universal's picture American-International rushed into release its variation, *The Amazing Colossal Man*. AIP followed this film with *The Spider* (1958), an effort to capitalize on the most thrilling sequence from *Shrinking Man*, Williams' deadly duel with the tarantula. By the end of the decade nearly every kind of animal, vegetable, or mineral had turned against man. Even gentle rain. In *The Monolith Monsters* (1957) water causes strange meteorites to multiply, growing into giant dominoes which thrive on the silicon content of human cells.

The fifties began quietly, with journeys to outer space undertaken every few months. Kurt Neumann launched his *Rocketship X-M* (1950) in June, while George Pal's more opulent *Destination Moon* (1950) reached us in August. The latter's single-frame animation and carefully designed models created a credible illusion of space travel which does not suffer much from comparison with the real thing encountered on television in the 1969 moon voyage of Apollo 11.

Neumann's ninety-five-thousand-dollar quickie of necessity sacrificed the special effects of *Destination Moon* to concentrate on the human element. RXM drifts off course to land on Mars, an astonishing replica of the California desert augmented by the sort of artificially constructed mountains Nathanael West found decorating the back lot as long ago as *The Day of the Locust.* Neither the unsettling discovery that Martian barbarians are remnants of a superior civilization eclipsed by atomic war nor the subsequent fatal crash of RXM in Nova Scotia deters the space program. At a press conference a bland government official announces without a trace of irony, "Tomorrow we start construction of RXM-2."

Cameron Mitchell found mini-skirted Marguerite Chapman living in an underground city in *Flight to Mars* (1951). Abbott & Costello fared even better in a Martian population consisting mostly of Miss Universe contestants in *Abbott and Costello Go To Mars* (1953). Civilization was rescued in *When Worlds Collide* (1951) by the rocket flight of forty selected survivors to the planet Zyra. For his Technicolor destruction of New York in a giant tidal wave, George Pal won an Oscar. Space travel declined somewhat thereafter to resume later in the decade under the topical stimulation of the American-Russian space race and the launching in October of 1957 of Sputnik.

No sooner had we probed the far places of the universe than reciprocal visits occurred. At first they were reassuring. The UFO's in *The Flying Saucer* (1950) weren't from outer space after all. And Klaatu, in Robert Wise's *The Day the Earth Stood Still* (1951), was a benevolent intruder only come to warn us to halt atomic testing or risk elimination from the galaxy as the most dangerously destructive planet in the universe. Succeeding aliens were not as high-minded as gently spoken Michael Rennie, or as admirably disciplined as his robot, Gort.

Sensational citings of Unidentified Flying Objects had begun in 1947. The Air Force developed intelligence programs for sorting out facts and fancies on what was rapidly becoming a public obsession. The wilder versions of escorted tours of the solar system could be dismissed out of hand, but many of the witnesses to saucer phenomena were reliable sorts, including a goodly number of experienced pilots, both civilian and military. In 1952 an Air Force major general stated that about 20 percent of documented UFO incidents involved "credible observers of relatively incredible things. We keep on being concerned about them."

In science fiction films, concern had long since passed over into the most horrific invasion of hostile aliens in the history of the movies. Often a feeling of helpless terror was generated less by the invading monsters than by the implication that conventional institutions were incapable of dealing with them. The UFO that crashed in the Arctic in *The Thing* (1951) carried aboard James Arness in the guise of an angry space creature resembling a walking carrot. Impractical scientists jeopardized human life in a foolish effort to preserve the thing for future study. But tough-minded Kenneth Tobey electrocuted it, reducing the eight-foot vegetable to a stewy puddle beyond academic interest. Scientist Robert Hutton had to be wrestled to the floor before military officer John Agar could render the *Invisible Invaders* (1959) visible with high frequency sound waves, thereby destroying them.

The loner with privileged knowledge of interplanetary invasion had a tough time of it. In Jack Arnold's *It Came from Outer Space* (1953), Richard Carlson has trouble convincing authorities that an extraterrestrial ship is buried in the desert. And Peter Graves escapes from hospital confinement to outrace his military superiors to a power generator on which the underground *Killers from Space* depend for life. Disturbed by his behavior, an FBI agent asks Graves' wife if he has "made any new friends lately—you know, not of the usual group."

Aliens were frequently hard for anyone to detect. They possessed simple farm animals in *The Beast With 1,000,000 Eyes* (1955), even a bridegroom in *I Married a Monster from Outer Space* (1958). Paul Birch, as the leader of an interplanetary expedition force, walked around in a blue suit and sunglasses in *Not of This Earth* (1957), as indistinguishable from the rest of us as any account executive on his way to lunch. Venerable John Agar, usually so trusty, was invaded by the diabolical half of the Manichean team of Gor and Vol in *The Brain from Planet Arous* (1957).

In a world where family pets turn viciously on their masters, where cows attack the farmers who come to milk them, and children run screaming from their own mothers, one's confidence in familiar allegiances naturally breaks down. A crank once wrote former Senator Thomas R. Kuchel to inform him of a plot on the part of thirty-five thousand disguised Chinese Communists to march across the border from Mexico to seize San Diego. Such craziness deserved understanding sympathy. On many nights the friendly streets outside the Fox Westwood looked suspiciously quiet, the psychic energy required to separate popular myth from public fact worn down at least until morning.

Invasion of the Body Snatchers (1956) is the classic presentation of the theme of alien possession, despite the emasculated ending Allied Artists forced on director Don Siegel. Kevin McCarthy returns to the small coastal town of Santa Mira to find various persons in the community psychotically fearful of members of their own families. The local psychiatrist acts as oblique historian, tying the peculiar fits to delusions "probably caused by response to what's going on in the world today." Soon the psychiatrist, too, is possessed, as are the police, McCarthy's close friend, a writer, and most of the

ALLIED ARTISTS
Invasion of the Body Snatchers: From left, King Donovan,
Carolyn Jones, Kevin McCarthy, and Dana Wynter variously
react to mysterious "pod person," part of one of the most
subtly invidious invasions from space in the decade's numerous
difficulties with interplanetary nastiness.

other townspeople. Pods drifting in from space re-form in
the image of individuals who are taken over in their sleep
by the invaders. It is a new world in which everybody is the
same, equally without the capacity for feeling.

The understated imagery of small-town life—hot-dog
stands, used-car lots, office buildings—is played off against
the mounting terror of a swift and final conversion produced
by "a malignant disease spreading throughout the country."
McCarthy and his girl, Dana Wynter, watch from a window
as people assemble around a truck in the town square, the
sort of gathering where you would expect to see farmers
selling produce fresh from the field. But this is no outdoor
market, and what is unloaded from the trucks isn't water-
melon but the giant pods being readied for distribution to
surrounding communities. A more chilling collision of the familiar with the sinister isn't to be found in fifties science
fiction.

"Keep your eyes wide and blank. Show no interest or ex-

citement," says McCarthy to Wynter as they plan their escape
through the square. But she nearly blows it when she screams
at the sight of a truck about to hit a running dog. In the final
scene of the movie, as Siegel intended it, McCarthy, alone
now, his woman a pod person, wanders crazed onto a free-
way, screaming to honking motorists, "They're here . . .
don't you see . . . they're here . . . you're next!" The film
was released early in the election year of 1956. By November
the pod people had handed the eggheads their second consecutive defeat, the Eisenhower blanket settling down around
us in a vote for four more years of undisturbed sleep.

Slushed on beer or cheap vodka and Neehi Orange, I saw
many science-fiction films from the back seat of a car in a
drive-in. Rock star Alice Cooper admits to saving his coins
when just a tyke to see the *Creature from the Black Lagoon.*
"Real horror can have more feeling than sex," he told
Rolling Stone in an interview. A Harvard philosopher adds,
"In horror movies, sexuality is not suggested but directly
coded onto, or synchronized with, the knives and teeth
as they penetrate." At sixteen or seventeen I would have
found both views a little effete, although I would not have
put my criticism of them exactly that way. Science-fiction
flicks were about the last film genre seen on a regular weekly
basis, the good and the bad a matter of ritual indifference.
They were the favorite films for dates. Monsters, however
flabby and retreaded their appearance, whether scaly like the
Creature, or metallic like *Kronos* (1957), or gelatinous like
The Blob (1958), produced feminine shudders which readily
escalated into sexual gropings rarely volunteered under ordinary dating conditions.

In the fifties families no longer went to the movies together.
Mom and Dad were home fitting the bubble to the new television set. We teen-agers went alone, choosing the pictures
most serviceable for the moment. In California in 1950 you

could drive across town in your own car at fourteen. The deep last rows of abandoned movie palaces in downtown Los Angeles held possibilities never imagined at twelve watching Roy Rogers at The Hitching Post.

With few exceptions, science fiction was watched with intermittent attentiveness, a condition owing less to our fatiguing sense of central focus than to the special uses we made of the movies. The camp sensibility, described so well by Susan Sontag in her seminal essay in 1964, was a widely shared possession in the fifties, although not yet delivered to us with the historical authority of the *Partisan Review*. *The Colossus of New York* (1958) was greatly admired for its wildly misfired intentions. A father tells the giant automaton in which his otherwise dead son's brain is encased, "Of course you'll never have a personal life—as a man!" But the colossus is amusingly unsuccessful at convincing its own metal parts of their sexual inability. Howls of laughter hardly subsided before the chromium offspring was taking hopeful peeps at Mala Powers in her nightgown, and disintegrating its own brother for making a pass at her.

Always excepting the uniquely benevolent Robby the Robot in *Forbidden Planet* (1956), only the *Creature from the Black Lagoon* joined that endearing tradition which includes Frankenstein and King Kong, monsters more sinned against than sinning. The Creature was continually put upon by scientists, who attempted, for purposes not always very clear, to remove him forcibly from his natural, primeval condition underwater. The Creature, for his part, always showed more than passing interest in whatever women were around— Julia Adams, Lori Nelson, or Leigh Snowden. In *Revenge of the Creature* he braved the dance floor of a Florida night-club, spiriting Lori Nelson away in the middle of a rock number in a frustrated attempt to return with her to his home in the water. Cheering the Creature in his abortive efforts to combat mid-fifties repression was, of course, just another way of voting thumbs-down on a society whose idea of scientific achievement was a freak exhibition of our scaly friend at a Miami marineland.

Jack Arnold directed the first two Creature films for Universal, but the mythic possibilities had been so richly developed that they carried through John Sherwood's more tepid conclusion to the trilogy, *The Creature Walks Among Us* (1956). In this last film the scientists are more odious than usual, Leigh Snowden a cheap tease hardly worthy of our beloved water monster's attention. The scientists cruelly alter the Creature, biologically alienating his body from its natural environment. He is placed in chains in a compound with land animals, an experience which understandably confuses and enrages him. The scientist most publicly devoted to disinterested pursuit of "reality and facts" kills the suspected lover of his wife, and throws the body into the Creature's cage in an effort to blame the murder on him. But the Creature escapes to dole out his own clumsy but unimprovable justice before heading for the ocean, his old home. In the last shot the Creature is seen loping down a hill toward the beach, unaware that science has made his instinctive return to the water a suicidal final journey.

An attraction of sci-fi flicks was the occasionally splendid special effects. The masterful tradition of single-frame animation perfected by Willis O'Brien was continued in the decade by his protege Ray Harryhausen. Edwin S. Porter had animated seven teddy bears as early as 1907, and O'Brien himself produced a five-minute prehistoric comedy *The Dinosaur and the Missing Link* in 1914, long before his famous King Kong appeared in the thirties. On O'Brien's three-year project, *Mighty Joe Young* (1949), Harryhausen did most of the actual animation work. O'Brien also worked on *The Black Scorpion* (1957), while Harryhausen created *The Beast From 20,000 Fathoms* and the giant Ymir in *20 Million Miles to Earth* (1957), the latter featuring an incredible sequence in which the baby monster is hatched from an egg. The most popular tabletop creation of the fifties was *Godzilla, King of the Monsters* (1956), produced by Japan's Toho Company and purchased for U.S. distribution for twelve thousand dollars by Joseph E. Levine, one of his first investments in the exploitation of inexpensively acquired foreign spectacles.

Poor technical effects ruined many sci-fi films, or quickly converted them into objects of hysterical amusement. Rear screen projection of the giant insects and lizards in *Killers from Space* was apparent even to the untrained eye. The destruction of aliens by nothing more convincing than the headlights of automobiles in *Invasion of the Saucer Men* (1957) was an outright admission of a dime-store budget. When *It! The Terror from Beyond Space* (1958) turned out to resemble our resurrected favorite, the Creature, we should have guessed that the richest veins already had been mined.

The fifties was the grand decade of the science-fiction film, just as the forties had been noted for horror pictures. Val Lewton died in 1951 about the time George Pal was colliding worlds. Lewton's intelligently eerie productions were among the most admired films of the forties, but the horror legacy to the succeeding decade was thin. American-International's teen-age monsters were immediate camp to everyone except the few critics who found them troubling symbols of alienated youth.

It remained for Hammer Films, a British company, to revive the classic horror film in 1957 with *The Curse of Frankenstein*. Although a small studio, Hammer produced with an eye for rich detail, including an eroticism not seen so openly in horror flicks since American films of the thirties. In addition to employing literate scripts, Hammer played off the understated performances of Peter Cushing and Christopher Lee against grisly pieces of business usually repressed in American films of the forties and fifties. In *Horror of*

Dracula (1958) the ritual shot of the stake being driven into the vampire's chest lingers beyond expectation. We see the stake enter the flesh, the blood curdling up through punctured clothing to puddle at the point of entry.

American movies, long censured in foreign countries for excessive brutality, usually drew the line at images of mutilation. Ironically, the new Hammer films were the most popular British entries in the American market since the Guinness comedies of the earlier fifties. By the end of the decade film students were discussing the choreography of violence in the famous shower scene in *Psycho* (1960). The unparalleled visual cruelty of many sixties movies engendered bitterly divided feelings. Cults developed for such otherwise different pictures as Roman Polanski's *Repulsion* (1965) and *The Night of the Living Dead* (1968). While some film buffs descanted on the poetry of blood, others waved their copies of *From Caligari to Hitler*, predicting impending neo-fascism advancing with each decapitation. Communities far from the cultural front responded to such independent *roughies* as *Blood Feast* (1963) by invoking rarely exercised censorship laws against violence.

10

$tars and $tudios

How bad was business, sweetie? So bad Army Archerd reported that Francis, the Talking Mule, was afraid to go near the Universal commissary. So bad an actress friend told Nina Foch, "Every lunchtime when I cross the Fox lot, I hope I make it to the fort before the Indians get me." At their annual awards dinner in 1958, the fearless screenwriters mounted a sketch called "The Bridge on the River Burbank," with Jack Benny as the tyrannical Colonel Sessue Warner. Confronting a group of writers held prisoners, Colonel Warner reminded them, "At RKO they're making bongo drums. Paramount has become a bottling plant for Coca-Cola. Universal is a storefront for Decca records. And at Fox they have so much oil they don't know where to bury their dead."

Hollywood—the city, not the state of mind—was considering spending $1,700,000 to revive its fading mythology. Tourists complained of arriving at Hollywood and Vine only to find fraternity boys teasing religious fanatics, who chalked sermons in the street while dirty papers scudded along the sidewalk in front of a drugstore which didn't even sell guides to the stars' homes. More Hollywood history was carved into the wooden booths at C. C. Brown's hot fudge palace than could be found in all the skidding night life between High-land and Western. Swells dining at Musso & Frank exited through the back to limousines waiting in the parking lot. They left Hollywood Boulevard to the wandering kids and confused tourists, who bumped their way through the parade of queens hustling from in front of Coffee Dan's east to the Las Palmas newsstand. At the Royal Room Jack Teagarden played while the beer drinkers lined up to take a leak in the one-stall men's room. In the middle of the week you could throw a stick of dynamite into most of the joints in Hollywood and nobody would be hurt.

Returning in 1958 from a two-year expatriation in Europe, Darryl F. Zanuck found the industry deep in gloom. Pro-duction was down from the three hundred and sixty pictures averaged annually in the early fifties to barely two hundred through the first eleven months of 1958. Early the next year, Samuel Goldwyn, speaking at the Screen Producers Guild, called conditions the worst he'd seen in his forty-seven years in the movie business. A few days later Cecil B. DeMille died of a heart attack at seventy-seven. He had predicted that his seventieth picture, *The Ten Commandments* (1956), would run for forty years.

Hollywood's previous period of despair had coincided with hard times for the entire country. In the thirties the customer had gone broke. The turbulent fifties was different. As one producer put it, "Hollywood is an island of depres-sion in a sea of prosperity. In the war there were not enough pictures. Now there are not enough customers." The hard facts were that motion picture production and distribution were no longer very good investments when measured against the potential in other industries. Before the war four out of five pictures returned their costs in U.S. bookings alone. By 1950 the number was one in ten. To make matters worse, after 1947 European governments developed various restrictions and taxations intended to tie up revenues earned on their shores. These "frozens assets" could be used only for investment in future pictures produced within the country doing the refrigerating. In effect, Hollywood was forced into partially subsidizing foreign film industries, consequently increasing its own inclination toward international roving.

At home the Justice Department extracted postwar consent decrees on an antitrust suit originally brought against the major studios in the thirties. Under the decrees the major production companies agreed to divest themselves of the giant theater chains through which they had controlled 80 percent of all urban first-run movie houses. Slowly, exhibitors were freed from the binds of "block booking," a form of industry force-feeding which required theaters to accept studio gruel in order to receive the rare servings of filet. Pictures were thrown onto an open and competitive market already battered by television into a precipitous decline of undetermined extent.

Without assurance that mediocre films would get sufficient bookings to be profitable, the studios cut back sharply on production, virtually eliminating the old program picture designed to hold hands with a cofeature of equally dubious attraction. The average cost of a movie, which already had doubled between 1940 and 1950, rose even higher as more eggs were risked in fewer baskets. Jack Warner expressed the communal wisdom when he said, "One picture at three million is a better investment than three at a million each." But the accountants' figures in annual stockholders' reports recorded the sobering facts about motion picture investment in the fifties. Corporate profit margins, which had reached 10 percent of gross revenues in 1946 and averaged nearly 7 percent throughout the forties, had shrunk by 1958–59 to slightly more than 3 percent. Other industries such as automobile manufacturing, tobacco, oil, drugs, or chemicals consistently averaged a 5 to 18 percent return on income. Among major industrial groups only food chains operated regularly on lower profit margins. This sad state of affairs prompted one wag to remark that the bananas in the late Carmen Miranda's hats were now a more profitable form of investment than the kind of movies in which she had so recently appeared.

Howard Hughes bought controlling interest in RKO from Floyd Odlum in 1948, and the studio lost twenty million dollars in the next five years. The payroll declined from two thousand to about five hundred in the same period. The most famous casualty was production chief Dore Schary, who was vexed into resigning when Hughes halted two of his projects—including plans for the war film *Battleground* (1949). Schary's resignation "saved me paying him two weeks' salary," Hughes reportedly said, and went on to sign up the "wonder boys," Jerry Wald and Norman Krasna. The well-advertised fifty million dollars' worth of pictures the two were to produce over the next five years never quite worked out. Of the sixty films contracted for only a handful was made, most notably Fritz Lang's *Clash by Night* (1952) and Nicholas Ray's *The Lusty Men* (1952).

RKO had the profitable Tarzan series, but lost its most lucrative independent product in 1953 when Walt Disney formed Buena Vista to distribute its own pictures. The more modest Filmakers, the company formed by Ida Lupino and Collier Young, also departed in 1953, with *The Hitch-Hiker* (a chilling exit piece and one of the sleepers of the year). RKO also handled a number of Samuel Goldwyn's lesser efforts, the most ambitious of which were *I Want You* and *Hans Christian Andersen* (1952). *The Thing* was a successful early entry in the science fiction genre, but the studio never again released anything similar. Busby Berkeley was engaged to enliven the dance sequences of *Two Tickets to Broadway,* but little with his signature on it reached the screen, not so much as one waltzing piano. RKO's high culture exhibits included the flop *Androcles and the Lion* (1952), and the more interesting Huntington Hartford anthology *Face to Face* (1952), for which James Agee scripted the segment "The Bride Comes to Yellow Sky."

Robert Mitchum and Jane Russell were RKO's principal attractions. Hughes personally supervised the career of the latter, complete with prodigious notes to Josef von Sternberg on how he wanted her breasts to look in *Macao* (1952). The long cycle of Mitchum thrillers beginning with *Out of the Past* (1947) and concluding with Preminger's *Angel Face* (1953) contains one of the most amusingly sustained screen images outside of Bogey in the forties.

Hughes' own projects were comical disasters. *Double Dynamite* was begun under a different title in 1948 and then fumbled with until its release three years later. The infamous *Jet Pilot* (1957) was on the runway so long it was ultimately released by Universal after Hughes had put RKO out of its misery in 1955 by selling out for twenty-five million to a subsidiary of General Tire.

Dore Schary brought *Battleground* from RKO to MGM where it grossed over seven million and stimulated a new cycle of war pictures. His predecessor as production chief at MGM was Louis B. Mayer, who was still around as vice-president in charge of studio operations. Conflict between the two was inevitable. In 1951 the Eastern money sided with Schary, and the parent company, Loew's Inc., bought Mayer out, retired him, and gave Schary a fifteen-year contract at two hundred thousand dollars a year with a sweetener of one hundred thousand shares of Loew's stock. Five years later Schary was gone, eased out, he told the press, because of his liberal political convictions. Over a year later stockholders were still mumbling about Schary's radical films, while the new Loew's president, Joseph R. Vogel, was calling the 1957 MGM product "the worst collection of pictures in its history."

Ironically, MGM's output under Schary was no more controversial than the other majors', productions under his personal supervision considerably less so than those made at Fox under Zanuck. Complaining in 1951 that Metro was out of touch with the national mood, William Poster of the *American Mercury* wrote, "American domestic life is habitually viewed by MGM as a kind of earthly paradise in which the American people as a whole participate." The reference was to an inherited tradition of sentimental family pictures and melodramatic star vehicles, opulent, glossy films made with a commanding pride in technical craft.

Well into the middle fifties, while others cut back costly overhead, MGM continued the most expensive contract list in the industry. Each year Esther Williams slipped into the water as the *Duchess of Idaho* (1950) or the *Million Dollar Mermaid* (1952); Lana Turner had her *Latin Lovers* (1953); Clark Gable tried *To Please a Lady* (1950) or was off *Across the Wide Missouri* (1951); and Elizabeth Taylor as *The Girl Who Had Everything* (1953) was growing up, learning that *Love Is Better Than Ever* (1952). No studio was more financially disrupted by the deterioration of the star system than MGM.

Under Schary, genre thrillers were rare, Huston's *The Asphalt Jungle* and the science-fiction sleeper *Forbidden Planet* standing out in brilliant isolation. Despite the success of *Battleground,* MGM made fewer war movies than either Warners or Fox. *Prisoner of War* (1954) dealt specifically with Korea, but apparently the indirection of *Go For Broke!* (1951) and *Take the High Ground!* (1953) was preferred. After Schary's departure the risky changing market was probed with adult pictures ranging in quality and intention from Richard Brooks' *The Brothers Karamazov* (1958) and *Cat on a Hot Tin Roof* to the sexual snickering of *It Started with a Kiss* (1959).

By 1957 only a third of the thirty Culver City stages was in use at any one time, and MGM was renting out half its facilities to independent producers. The studio was well in the red that year. To regain its fading grandeur it returned to one of its earliest successes, a triumph dating back to 1925. At fifteen million the new *Ben-Hur* (1959) was the most expensive picture in history, with a three-million-dollar promotional budget and a Sindlinger and Company survey of national recognition to see if the advertising was working. It was. Half the people in the country had heard of the film before its release. Four paperback publishers loaded news-stands with a million copies of Lew Wallace's 1880 novel, and Schrafft's promised the first new candy bar in a decade, a chocolate "Ben-Hur" to melt in sweaty hands during the famous chariot race. The film pulled MGM out of several years of deficit gloom, but continued a fatal trend toward suicidal budgets.

Under Darryl F. Zanuck, Fox's films of the earlier fifties were gutsier and more visceral than MGM's, although Spyros Skouras' extensive commitment to CinemaScope paved the way for the shoot-the-studio gamble on spectaculars which led to *Cleopatra* (1963) and a bath of red ink throughout the sixties. As early as 1959 the fascination with size instead of quality had reduced net income to 2.3 million, down from 7.6 million the year before and over 8 million in 1954, CinemaScope's rosiest first year of profits.

With Clifton Webb comedies and Betty Grable musicals for family fare, Fox answered Schary's *Battleground* with Zanuck's *Twelve O'Clock High* (1949), unleashed Samuel Fuller's brutally tough *Fixed Bayonets* (1951), and produced a civilized sleeper in Henry Hathaway's *The Desert Fox* (1951), with James Mason as Rommel. Zanuck's personal productions ranged from the unpopular *No Way Out* through the controversial *Viva Zapata!* (1952) to the wide screen banality of *The Egyptian* (1954). Fox directors included such established craftsmen as Otto Preminger and the versatile Henry Hathaway, as well as the socially conscious Elia Kazan, and, briefly, that energetic precursor of the Pop Sensibility, Frank Tashlin.

Marilyn Monroe, whose previous Fox option had been dropped, returned to the studio almost by accident for *All About Eve*. According to Joseph L. Mankiewicz, her agent, Johnny Hyde, convinced a reluctant Zanuck to agree to Monroe in the part of George Sanders' protege, "a graduate of the Copacabana School of Dramatic Arts." Fox had comparative good luck with newcomers, developing such personalities as Jean Peters, Jeff Hunter, Mitzi Gaynor, and Robert Wagner. And if May Britt failed to achieved the hoped-for cross between Dietrich and Monroe, she was, at least, not as blandly undistinguished as Columbia's Anthony Dexter, who went from *Valentino* (1951) directly to pirate ships from which he never returned.

When Zanuck departed to go into independent production, his successor at Fox, Buddy Adler, attempted to keep the studio flexibly in touch with the fragmenting market through science-fiction films like *The Fly* (1958) and youth-oriented pictures such as *Bernardine* (1957) with Pat Boone. Studio prestige rode rather unevenly on movies like *The Young Lions* (1958) and *The Diary of Anne Frank* (1959), while cultural lag was sumptuously evident in *South Pacific* in Todd-AO.

Warners, famous for its survival sense of economy, moved more quickly toward independent production than either Fox or MGM. By 1953 nearly half its output was from independents. And in 1957 fewer than one in three of its releases was studio produced, compared to over 40 percent at Fox and over 50 percent at Metro. Riding the crest of James Dean's popularity and the successes of *Mister Roberts* (1955) and *The Searchers* (1956), Warners reported a net profit in excess of seventeen million for 1956, one of the

finest years enjoyed by any studio in the decade. Earlier in
the summer an Eastern syndicate led by Serge Semenenko, a
senior vice-president of the First National Bank of Boston,
bought effective control of Warners, although Jack Warner
remained as president, and with over two hundred thousand
shares the largest single stockholder.

New faces replaced old in the shifting fifties at Warners.
Bogart left to pursue independent production, Bette Davis
in a search for better parts, Joan Crawford and Barbara
Stanwyck to face the uncertainty of free-lance demand for
mature feminine leads. James Dean flashed talent briefly,
Tab Hunter not at all. Director Michael Curtiz, of *Casa-
blanca* (1943) fame, went back with Warners to *The Third
Degree* in 1927. He continued through the decade, an ex-
emplary master of the studio system which required traveling
with ease from *Young Man with a Horn* (1950) at Warners,
to *White Christmas* (1954) at Paramount, and then on to
The Proud Rebel (1958), a Disney release. Mervyn LeRoy
returned from MGM to handle such popular prestige items
as *The Bad Seed* (1956) and *The FBI Story* (1959). Directorial debuts of varying significance were made by Jack
Webb with *Dragnet* (1954) and Arthur Penn with *The
Left-Handed Gun* (1958).

Warners historic, if mostly illusory, role as Hollywood's
social conscience paled to insignificance in the fifties. *Storm
Warning* (1951) patronized the audience in exposing the
menace of the Ku Klux Klan, a subject the studio had treated
with more intelligence in the thirties with *Black Legion*
(1937). *A Lion Is in the Streets* (1953), despite James
Cagney in the role of the southern demagogue, was an un-
convincingly melodramatic replay of Columbia's *All the
King's Men* (1949). Elia Kazan's *A Face in the Crowd*
(1957) was an early dramatization of the power of media
hype, and indicated an emerging source of political image-
making no further away than the Presidential election of
1960. But clearly the film was more important as a devel-

opment in Kazan's career than as an index of enlightened studio policy in the late fifties.

Paramount entered the decade with a firm hold on genre entertainment of a solidly profitable and decidedly uncontroversial nature. Production from the early fifties was about evenly split between independents and studio projects. The Williams, Pine and Thomas, escalated from modest forties thrillers into costlier swashbuckling, often with John Payne and Rhonda Fleming, and always with plenty of swords and torn shirts. Cecil B. DeMille handled the really big stuff, with the more than fourteen million spent on *The Ten Commandments* the top budget in Paramount history. Alfred Hitchcock was in his sunny middle register with *To Catch a Thief* and *The Man Who Knew Too Much* (1956), and George Pal to everyone's delight destroyed the world several times over.

Bob Hope, Bing Crosby, and Martin & Lewis gave the

PARAMOUNT
Stalag 17: William Holden and Otto Preminger in campy pose for production still for Billy Wilder's boffo World War II prison camp film.

studio four of the most popular talents for breezy flicks in movie history, while Billy Wilder was a reminder of the sophistication associated with Paramount comedies from Lubitsch through Preston Sturges. Under production chiefs Don Hartman and Y. Frank Freeman war pictures were in low profile, with Wilder's direction of Preminger in *Stalag 17* (1953) the apotheosis of high camp. Topical subjects seldom explored beyond *The Search for Bridey Murphy* (1956), although Owen Crump's Korean documentary, *Cease Fire*, brought Paramount into one of its rare altercations with the Production Code. William Alland's bid for the teenage market was mild compared to the going rate.

Paramount introduced Charlton Heston in *Dark City* (1950), and Steven McQueen, as he was then known, survived *The Blob* (1958) nearly alone in a cast distinguished by talents even more modest than Jack H. Harris' two-hundred-thousand-dollar budget. Carol Ohmart received a careful buildup, including the usual *Life* puffery, for her debut in *The Scarlet Hour* (1956), but it was becoming nearly impossible for studios to find enough inexpensive properties through which to develop gradually new stars. As at the other majors high culture consisted of stuffing and mounting fancy Broadway catches. However, *The Rose Tattoo* (1955), *The Rainmaker* (1956), and *Desire Under the Elms* (1958) looked more like earnestly displayed trophies than most.

Considerably downstream from the "big five," Universal fished its same old spot well into the decade. Profits tripled between 1950 and 1954 as the studio firmly rejected the drift toward urban sophistication, independent production, and controversial stories. When Universal went book buying it came up with novels by Howard Pyle and Rex Beach—its moderns were Lloyd C. Douglas and Edison Marshall. The gamiest novel it handled was Irving Shulman's *The Amboy Dukes*, licked into shape in 1949 as *City Across the River*.

Shortly thereafter, Decca Records acquired control, and under Milton R. Rackmil Universal remained steadfastly committed to films for the nabes, the small-town and rural sensibility which clung to Abbot & Costello; the Kettles; Francis, the Talking Mule; and the Bonzo pictures, while waiting for television prices to come into the range of more modest budgets.

While the majors reduced contract lists, Universal successfully developed its own younger talent—Jeff Chandler, Tony Curtis, Rock Hudson. Sandra Dee, entirely invented by Ross Hunter out of the usable parts of teen-age model Alexandra Zuck, was the studio's contribution to the humanoid style in fifties glamour. Hunter's real genius, however, was to recognize in the fragmenting audience a segment insufficiently exploited by the majors—the ladies' matinee crowd. The weepies found a friend in Hunter. He skillfully embalmed former stars, dressed them in fashion-show wardrobes, and yet held tight rein on the costs of such pictures as *Magnificent Obsession* (1954) and *Imitation of Life* (1959).

By the mid-fifties earnings had plateaued, and in 1956 Universal entered the adult market with a rush of problem pictures unlike anything it had done since the late forties. Esther Williams was exposed to the dry-land dangers of a sexual psychopath in *The Unguarded Moment* (1956), and the rest of us to corrupt unions in *Slaughter on Tenth Avenue*, alcoholics in *Voice in the Mirror* (1958), and Doris Day's peculiar case of terminal virginity in *Pillow Talk*. Independents like Kirk Douglas' Bryna Productions were welcome for the first time in 1958, and the nine million spent on *Spartacus* was tops in studio history. In a more modest price range were the science-fiction films of Jack Arnold, arguably the most inventive work to come out of Universal in the fifties.

In his last nine years on earth rough tough Harry Cohn saw his Columbia Pictures win the Oscar for Best Film four times—*All the King's Men* (1949), *From Here to Eternity* (1953), *On the Waterfront* (1954), and *The Bridge on the River Kwai* (1957). The studio grossed fifty-nine million in 1950 and nearly twice that amount at the end of the decade, more, in fact, than either Warners or Paramount and only a few million less than Fox.

In Kim Novak, Cohn created the last studio-developed sex symbol of any significance. The advertising for her debut in *Pushover* (1954) described her as "what the boys have been waiting for." Cohn called her a "fat Polack." But then he called Judy Holliday a "fat ass," hauled Rita Hayworth into court for failing to appear for a movie the studio never made, and was blasted by Arlene Dahl, who sued Columbia for a million dollars over "lewd, lascivious, and obscene" ads for her film *Wicked as They Come* (1957). Cohn regularly greeted Broderick Crawford with the salutation, "Fuck you, for openers!" Actors tended to duck when he spoke. With writers it was a somewhat different matter. Reportedly, he paid Garson Kanin a million bucks for *Born Yesterday* (1950). He tried to save Sidney Buchman from the blacklist. And to Daniel Taradash he fulfilled an unprofitable promise to film *Storm Center*, a sure loser as the only attack on the HUAC ever made in a Hollywood studio.

F. Scott Fitzgerald once said that the mark of an intelligent man was that he could hold two opposing ideas in his head simultaneously and function. Cohn's approach to independent production illustrated a variation on the theme. Stanley Kramer and Jungle Sam Katzman often passed each other in the hall, the one on his way to producing *Death of a Salesman* (1951), *The Sniper*, or *The Member of the Wedding* (1952); the other off to check Johnny Weissmuller's wardrobe for a Jungle Jim flick. In 1957 Katzman claimed that none of the more than 110 pictures he'd done for Columbia had lost money. *Rock Around the Clock* knocked down four million alone. Kramer, by contrast, seldom made a profitable picture for Cohn. His own musical, *The 5,000 Fingers of Dr. T.* (1953), lost well over a million.

Ordinarily Cohn watched costs with a jeweler's eye for detail. He prided himself on miraculously holding the budget for *From Here to Eternity* to under two million. His personal spree was combining Frank Sinatra with Cohn's two greatest creations, Rita Hayworth and Kim Novak, in *Pal Joey*. Still, in days when budgets were rising to ten million and beyond, Columbia spent less than five million on its most expensive film ever, *They Came to Cordura* (1959).

Cohn founded Columbia in 1924. When he died at sixty-six in 1958, he had seen the studio rise from Poverty Row to take its place as a major influence in the industry, its prestige pictures gutsier than were characteristic of the fading old-line majors. Even such smaller films as Nicholas Ray's *In a Lonely Place*, Fritz Lang's *The Big Heat* (1953), Don Siegel's *The Lineup*, Irving Lerner's *Murder by Contract*, and Samuel Fuller's *The Crimson Kimono* (1959) were among the decade's most interesting examples of the unpretentiously enduring suspense picture.

When lawyers Robert Benjamin and Arthur B. Krim sat down to play the piano at United Artists, everybody laughed. UA had no stars, no studio, and no pictures. It was losing one hundred thousand dollars a week. Revenues for 1950 were less than at Universal or Republic, and not much more than at inconsequential Monogram. Spyros Skouras slipped the pair a five-hundred-thousand-dollar personal loan because he thought it would be bad for industry morale if a company as once prominent as UA went under.

After eight years with Krim as president and Benjamin chairman of the board, United Artists' income had increased more than 400 percent to nearly the 100 million mark. In a period of remarkable instability net income improved each year between 1951 and 1959. At the end of the decade, UA, apart from the also rapidly growing Disney, was the only company whose stock was widely regarded as an attractive investment by such financial services as Dow Jones and Standard & Poor's.

United Artists made no films of its own. It distributed the work of independent producers for whom, usually, it also arranged financing. With no studio overhead and no expensive contract list, UA could bring pictures in at prices well below most of the competition. *Fortune* estimated that the three-hundred-thousand-dollar budget for *The Moon Is Blue* would have doubled at a major studio. As power shifted from the harried studios to independent talent, UA developed a tradition of providing "creative autonomy," as well as a large piece of the action, for such production companies as The Associates and Aldrich, Hecht-Hill-Lancaster, Joseph L. Mankiewicz' Figaro Inc., Gregory Peck's Melville Productions, John Wayne's Batjac Productions, Frank Sinatra's Kent Productions, Hope Enterprises, and many others. Top stars could demand between 30 and 75 percent of the net profit from packages they produced to be distributed by United Artists.

From the first important winner acquired by Benjamin and Krim—*The African Queen* (1951)—on, the output through UA was astonishing: *The Barefoot Contessa* (1954), *Beat the Devil* (1954), *Marty* (1955), *The Big Knife, Attack!, Sweet Smell of Success* (1957), *Twelve Angry Men* (1957), *Paths of Glory, Witness for the Prosecution* (1957), *Some Like It Hot* (1959), and so forth. And even this list omits such prized sleepers as *Actors and Sin* (1952) and *Suddenly* (1954), as well as those forgotten early films of Stanley Kubrick and Robert Altman, *Killer's Kiss* (1955) and *The Delinquents* (1957).

While Disney specialized in the family trade and American-International mined the drive-in crowd, United Artists distributed adult pictures for mature audiences of whatever age. Each proved that films aimed at defined segments within the pluralistic postwar mass were more consistently profitable than bland movies intended for the old undifferentiated general audience. Robert Benjamin summarized UA's philosophy by saying, "I like to think that in our years at UA there will be perhaps a dozen pictures made that wouldn't have been made if we weren't around." And producer-director Robert Aldrich, more than once beneficiary of that attitude, added that independents had taught the old-line studios how to turn out good pictures at a reasonable price.

The successful rise of American-International already has been discussed. Of the demise of Republic and the transmutation of Monogram into Allied Artists little needs to be said. In the late forties Herbert J. Yates, president and founder of Republic, told a New York *Herald Tribune* reporter, "We don't give a damn for artistic integrity." It was a pledge Republic almost never violated. In early 1958 the studio, which had produced no films of its own for several years, began to dismantle its operations. "The sooner, the better," said Yates, no doubt remembering better days when Robert Rockwell, Penny Edwards, and his wife, Vera Hruba Ralston, held their own among Saturday afternoon faithfuls.

In 1953 Monogram recognized that the program picture was finished and attempted to erase its past image as a B factory by taking on the name of its own subsidiary, Allied Artists. Lindsley Parsons provided low-key thrillers and William Castle amusing hokum. Walter Wanger and Don Siegel combined to produce the excellent *Riot in Cell Block 11* (1954) and *Invasion of the Body Snatchers*. Joseph H. Lewis' *The Big Combo* (1955) and Phil Karlson's *The Phenix City Story* (1955) were also admired. Larger budgets and more prestigious properties were undertaken with William Wyler's *Friendly Persuasion* (1956) and Billy Wilder's *Love in the Afternoon* (1957). In the last three years of the decade Allied lost more than three million dollars, and produced revenues even worse than those of the rapidly sinking Republic, with which it had once had more pleasant things in common.

As the CinemaScope opiate wore off, new demons were summoned forth to explain the continuing high percentage of losing pictures. By the late fifties, with more than half of all film production independent, more than half of all films were also losing money. In 1957 *Life* discovered a New Hollywood in which the stars in various combinations with powerful agents, producers, and directors were dictating packages to the studios. The result was fantastic salaries and unprecedented participation. To the studios this was up against the wall, your money or your life. Samuel Goldwyn predicted that for stars "these demands can mean only their own self-destruction ultimately." Producer Arthur Hornblow Jr. labeled rising salaries "vanity badges" and called them the "curse of the motion picture business." Gary Cooper said the studios had created their own Frankensteins and then abandoned them, forcing talent to contract individually for survival.

Stars with long memories or good history teachers recalled the early exploitation of screen actors by less than benevolent studios. Before 1910 there were no film credits for screen actors. Paternalistic Biograph insisted that players "renounce their names when they join the company." Without the interest of movie magazines and film fans, "picture players" never would have become "stars." Now the power had shifted decisively. Weakened studios had to bid for the talent whose record carried muscle at the bank.

Even stars still under long-term contract grew restless. Kim Novak refused to report to work for *Vertigo* (1958) under her 1955 Columbia contract of twelve hundred and fifty dollars a week. Otto Preminger had paid Columbia one hundred thousand dollars for her loan-out services in *The Man With the Golden Arm*. Symbolic of the new power alignment was the William Morris Agency, Novak's agent, explaining the facts of life to Harry Cohn. Monroe walked out on Fox, and many believe her antics on the ill-fated *Something's Got to Give* reflected a wild personal sabotage of the studio's effort to extract two final pictures from her at one hundred thousand dollars each under her old 1956 contract.

From the modest 30 to 50 percent of the net offered by Universal to James Stewart and Tyrone Power in the early fifties demands rose as rapidly as the mercury in a thermometer under direct assault of a blowtorch. For *Boy on a Dolphin* (1957) Alan Ladd got two hundred ninety thousand dollars plus a box on which to stand in two-shots so that he wouldn't always seem to be peering into the Amazonian bosom of the much taller Sophia Loren. For *On the Beach* Ava Gardner received four hundred thousand dollars plus a grand a week for incidentals. Tony Curtis wanted and got 10 percent of the gross for *The Defiant Ones.*

William Holden's fabled deal for *The Bridge on the River Kwai* worked out to a deferred salary of well over two million paid out at the rate of fifty thousand dollars a year for the rest of his life. *Suddenly, Last Summer* brought Elizabeth Taylor five hundred thousand dollars and 10 percent of the gross. Less than a year later Army Archerd announced that her current fee was a cool million. Her contract for *Cleopatra* ran to pages of expensive fine-print conditions, in addition to 10 percent of the gross and fifty thousand dollars a week after the first sixteen weeks of shooting.

Unfortunately, this suicidal trend appeared sound business to many of the participants. The star is the single most important element in a film and always will be, explained Tony Curtis. "Nobody is going to give me 10 percent of the gross because he thinks I look good in shorts," he reasoned. Still, it didn't hurt to try. In 1959 the agent for Sarita Montiel, a Spanish actress of noble proportions and uncertain talent, was around town asking for $350,000 plus 50 percent of the net. She looked great in shorts.

11
The Tit
Culture

All the sailors in *The Deep Six* (1958) agreed on the prize entry in Joey Bishop's little black book. It was a lady with a thirty-nine-inch bust, her name underlined in red. As early as 1946 André Bazin noted that "American eroticism—and hence cinematic eroticism—seems to have moved in recent years from the leg to the bosom." A chief architect of the new national obsession was Howard Hughes, who discovered Jane Russell in a dentist's office, designed a special brassiere for her, and assigned cinematographer Lucien Ballard to give her a screen test. Realizing, as Ballard put it, that Hughes "had a thing for tits," the cameraman through skillful crosslighting emphasized the famous Russell bulwark. "Hughes went wild for it," Ballard said. "He had the scene made into a loop, and he'd run it over and over again."

The forties was the decade for legs. Betty Grable was the favorite GI pinup, and her most famous pose showed her from the backside, smiling over her shoulder at the camera. The first thing George Murphy wanted to see when Carole Landis entered his office in *The Powers Girl* (1943) was a flash of her pins. Virginia Mayo in *The Girl From Jones Beach* (1949) and Joan Caulfield in *The Petty Girl* (1950) typified the leggy look of the famous *Esquire* artist. *Sweater Girl* (1942) was glaringly misnamed. June Preisser wore the title garment the way a coat hanger does. With *The Outlaw* (1943) Howard Hughes made sure the same mistake never occurred again.

While the nation went to war, Hughes conducted his own independent campaign against the Production Code, which as early as 1940 had begun to interfere with his plans to immortalize Jane Russell. Before shooting on *The Outlaw* began, the PCA raised twenty-three objections to the script. After a print was previewed in early 1941, Joseph Breen fired off an uncustomary letter to his boss, Will Hays, outlining the obvious intent of Hughes' picture. "In my more than ten years of critical examination of motion pictures I have never seen anything quite so unacceptable as the shots of the breasts of the character Rio. . . . Throughout almost half the picture the girl's breasts, which are quite large and prominent, are shockingly uncovered." Exactly. And publicist Russell Birdwell was given the job of seeing that the public was made well aware of the fact.

A Jane Russell billboard, the likes of which had never been seen along a public thoroughfare, went up in San Francisco and Los Angeles. The haystack on which Russell lies is sketched in as obliquely as the background for a UPA cartoon. All the action is in the torso. The skirt is shucked back to the point of oblivion, the legs arched, just enough tension exerted from the balls of the feet to tighten the calf muscles in that long erotic arc familiar to generations of Cheesecake fans. Up above is the magnificent Russell cleavage, the right breast barely contained at the nipple as the dress sags away under the terrific weight and a sliding shoulder strap. In Russell's right hand is a menacing six-shooter, on her face the bland ambiguous pout of a pop Mona Lisa. Darryl F. Zanuck called the billboard "a disgrace to the industry." Today, photographs of it are a collector's item.

The Outlaw premiered in 1943 in San Francisco. Immediately, it developed the reputation as a hot number among servicemen drifting along Market Street in search of pleasant memories to go with their three-day passes. On certain evenings the sound track couldn't be heard for more than a few minutes at a stretch, the spontaneous military salute to the Russell bazooms frequently more witty than the dialogue anyway. The police busted the film, some say as part of a graduated plan of sensationalism designed by Hughes himself. At any rate, Judge Twain Michaelson refused to believe the citizenry was corrupted into "lewdness and licentiousness" and dismissed the case in Municipal Court.

Suddenly, the picture disappeared, returned mysteriously to Hughes headquarters at 7000 Romaine Avenue in Los Angeles. A sanctuary with lead walls was constructed for the original negative and there it remained until the end of the war. The MPAA took a dim view of the advertising submitted to it prior to the re-release of the film. When Hughes disregarded its suggestions, it rescinded the previously granted Seal.

How Would You Like To Tussle With Russell? one piece of promotional copy asked. The crowd for the Los Angeles opening answered by arriving early in the morning, wax paper and napkins from portable breakfasts littering the sidewalk before noon. Late arrivals brought bagged lunches and the determination to stick it out on line until they learned, as another piece of advertising put it, "the two great reasons for Jane Russell's rise to stardom."

The Outlaw became the mythic "dirty movie," and like most myths, what the culture does with them is more important than the exact historical circumstances from which they emerge. In 1945 I was thrown out of a theater because the manager cleared the place of minors before he would allow the tepid and inoffensive *Earl Carroll Vanities* (1945) to be projected. That was the forties for you. *The Outlaw,* in focusing the American imagination on the bosom, belonged more to the erotic subterfuges bubbling through minor flicks of the fifties than to its own more innocent decade. When I finally saw the film, more than ten years after Hughes had started production, it had long since become one of the secret rites of manhood, an event strategically placed somewhere between the first shave and the first fumble at losing one's virginity. Adults remembered the picture, too. As late as 1954, in another RKO movie, *Susan Slept Here*, Dick Powell replied to Debbie Reynolds' histrionic pretense that she was an actress, "Yeah, I saw you in *The Outlaw*."

Hughes' great cultural contribution was what Murray Schumach called "mammary madness," the most extravagant exploitation of the female figure in the history of the game. The movies never could have done it alone. The bosom fetish had conspirators at every level of the culture. Among strippers of the forties, the mammothly endowed Carrie Finnell was a comedy act, tassels revolving at high speed in opposite directions. Tempest Storm, the new star of the fifties, presumably was not a joke. And students of comic art can trace the development of Al Capp's Daisy Mae from the flat-chested original of 1934, through the burgeoning forties, and into the pneumatic fifties when she finally resembles one of the buxom interchangeable parts in the new men's magazines.

According to the inventive captions of *Titter* and *Wink* all the models were starlets. Edgar Morin makes a useful distinction between a pinup and a starlet. The former is simply a girl who appears in men's magazines, frequently under a variety of pseudonyms. A starlet, while making the same rounds, retains a name and identity, and at least the faint suggestion of a movie career. Busty Brown and Betty Blue were pinups, but Mara Corday and Irish McCalla were starlets. The trip was never easy passage and seldom one way. The girlie mags booming into circulation in the postwar years were the most insistent exponents of the breast fetish, the starlets exploited by them the brief objects of an obsession we know less about than we do the tribal habits of the Trobriand Islanders.

One of the most popular and influential of the pre-*Playboy* men's magazines was *Night and Day*. Begun in the late forties, it had a circulation of nearly 750,000 by the early fifties. Readers hoarded copies. In Europe and England back issues sold at a premium, wily continentals sensing something eccentrically American in the bosomy icons of "America's Picture Magazine of Entertainment." The entertainment in *Night and Day* was a decade-long celebration of the tit culture.

Most of the models wanted to be in the movies, like the "14-year-old marvel with the overflow figure," Marlinda Lee Fitzgerald, whose bust size was nearly three times her age. Some of them made it, after a fashion. A 1957 beauty contest carried the breast fetish to a high point of surreal dehumanization. Readers were asked to select the most attractively developed bust from a group of twenty-seven photographs in which only the contestant's bosom appeared. Distracting faces, arms, legs, and other esthetically unimportant portions of anatomy were carefully cropped from each shot. The winner of "the most successful competition ever run" by *Night and Day* was Meg Myles, a starlet, of course, whose movie career up to that time consisted of a a walk through in *The Phenix City Story* (1955). Anita Ekberg was a distant second, with Monique Von Vooren, Virginia Bell, and even Sophia Loren scattered far behind.

Magazines like *Night and Day, Peep Show, Pix, Modern Man, Xcitement*, and dozens of others projected an image of female sexuality in which eroticism was displaced from the whole woman into the component parts. The sleazier magazines concentrated on a hard cocktail-waitress look: platinum hair, huge breasts, rotary engine rump packed into metallic toreadors and stiletto heels. The archetypes were starlets like Mamie Van Doren, Mari Blanchard, and Barbara Nichols, most of whom had begun their careers as pinups in the girlie mags. These were women formed for the world of motorcycles and hot rods, gangsters and gang bangs, swinger bars and motel orgies. In the movies their sexual attraction was sharply qualified by their profound threat to the domestic ideal. You could never imagine them happily married and raising families in the suburbs.

Audrey Totter in *Tension* (1949) exemplified the type. She mouthed a hamburger at a drugstore lunch counter while poring over pictures in a movie magazine. Her husband, Richard Basehart, is the mild manager of the place, economizing with a one-room apartment, a dutiful American Joe deferring pleasure to get ahead. He even works at night, a mistake as evident as his wife's tightly packed sweaters.

The postwar tit queen is too restless for a life measured out in installment buying and overtime. "It was different in San Diego. You were kind of cute in your uniform," Totter tells her husband. He attempts to appease her appetite for luxury by purchasing a tract home. Totter complains that it's "thirty minutes from nowhere." Told that the FHA already has approved the loan, she replies, "Let them live there, then." Small wonder that Basehart soon has murder on his mind.

Murder and sex often are inextricable in the tit culture. *Niagara* (1953) was Marilyn Monroe's most graphic depiction of the men's mag fantasy. With lipstick thick enough to chew, she rolled around inside her blouse with sensual contempt for conventional undergarments. Women who abandoned bras in the fifties were never up to much good. Jean Peters, as a demure newlywed, provided an acceptably subdued contrast to Monroe. She may have been the girl next door, but Monroe was the woman men dreamed about in the pages of *Titter* and *Wink*. Naturally, she wanted to murder her husband.

Niagara includes an amusingly classic reference to fifties breast fetish. Peters' husband wants to take a photo of his new bride in her sunsuit on the patio of their motel. "Let's have a profile," he says, and she gently turns her head to the side. "No," he chuckles, indicating with his hands that he means cheesecake, a profile of her breasts. Peters dutifully scoots to a sideways position on the chaise. "Now take a deep breath," her husband commands. Just as he sights her image through the viewfinder of his camera, a dark shadow falls across Peters' figure, ruining the picture. It is the shadow of Marilyn Monroe.

The immediate legacy of *Niagara* was Jayne Mansfield, who grotesquely caricatured the Monroe part in a way Marilyn courageously resisted in her own career. She aped the quotable Monroe with gaffes as spontaneous as a press agent's release. "I love turkey, especially when it's cooked," she once said. More probably her own was her comment that Jean Harlow's life reminded her "of that beautiful poem by Kelly and Sheats about the athlete who died young." Just as Marilyn reportedly wanted to play in a movie version of *The Brothers Karamazov,* Mansfield opted for *The Magic Mountain.* "I want to play the lead," she said. The lead was Hans Castorp, a man. Nobody thought to ask her if she had in mind playing the mountain itself.

At Fox Mansfield heard rumors that she was being groomed as a possible replacement for the increasingly difficult Monroe. Sheree North had worked *How to Be Very, Very Popular* (1955) when Marilyn rejected the picture. Modest Sheree admitted that Marilyn "takes a bigger lead off first base than I do." By that criterion, Mansfield could steal second without moving an inch.

Frank Tashlin directed Mansfield in her first important film, *The Girl Can't Help It.* In it Jayne, a bottle of milk clutched to each breast, confronted Tom Ewell at his apartment door. "Are these yours?" she asked the befuddled

Ewell. Tashlin correctly saw that Mansfield, in herself, was
a bizarre cultural comment on the erotic hang-ups of the
fifties. Her energetic ineptitude was a comic gift of sorts.
Used carelessly, she lost the fine edge of self-parody which
was her single intuitive gift.

Tashlin herded her through *Will Success Spoil Rock Hun-*
ter? (1957), in which she was played off against the modestly
endowed Betsy Drake. Tony Randall, as Drake's boyfriend,
was so taken with the Mansfield bombas that poor Betsy
undertook painful exercises to expand her bosom. Many
critics found the joke in poor taste, although, in characteristic
Tashlin manner, it was unfailingly observant of the pop madness of the moment. After *Rock Hunter* Mansfield's career
at Fox was mostly downhill. *The Wayward Bus* (1957) had
already proved that she couldn't project the vulnerable eroticism of Monroe in *Bus Stop*. Years later, Tommy Noonan's
nudie *Promises, Promises* (1963) exposed more than the
disappointing sag of Mansfield's flesh. In the sixties Jayne

20TH CENTURY-FOX
Will Success Spoil Rock Hunter?: Joan Blondell helps Jayne Mansfield
translate from the Metalious.

was no longer amusing. The real star of the film was T. C. Jones—a female impersonator.

Sociologists Martha Wolfenstein and Nathan Leites discovered in the films of the forties a recurrent feminine type which they called the "good-bad girl." These ladies, of whom Rita Hayworth as *Gilda* (1946) was prototypic, were sexually exciting women who appeared promiscuous or worse until near the final scenes. At picture's end their essential innocence was asserted no matter what appearances previously had suggested. According to the sociologists it was a ritual way of joining in one image forbidden ideas of carnality and traditional demands for the good virgin mother would like.

Among sex starlets Mamie Van Doren most persistently played the "good-bad girl" of the fifties. Only by then the demand for good virgins was entering a long bear market. Mamie was gum chewing, hip talking, and city tough. Beginning with *Running Wild* (1955) the rock and delinquency

WARNERS
Untamed Youth: Mamie Van Doren entertains a group of the untamed—a project which occupied her throughout most of the fifties.

cycles fused in a series of strange pictures in which Mamie faced a cruel world armed mostly with a body she had learned to use the way a hunter uses a steel trap. Some of these films are at least of anthropological curiosity.

In *Untamed Youth* (1957) Mamie was sentenced to a corrupt work farm with sister Lori Nelson. The kids at Tropp Ranch are cool. It's the authorities charged with their rehabilitation who are "untamed." A Presley imitator in an Ivy League cap with a buckle in the back sums up the social conflict in a song: "You can make me sing, you can make me dance/Make me rock right out of my pants, but you ain't gonna make a cotton picker out of me." Mamie, however, is not rocked out of her pants. The evil ranch operator, John Russell, attempts to "audition" her only to discover that her education stopped short at the definition of euphemism.

Mamie was in trouble again in *Girls Town* (1959). Taking a rap for her kid sister, she is consigned to a home for wayward girls run by nuns but secretly controlled by a clutch of dykes. It's the sort of irony that goes a long way toward explaining Mamie's unconcealed contempt for square society. When the dykes haul her before a mock court, she tells the most repulsive of them, "Why don't you go bingle your bongle?"

For film freaks the Van Doren flicks were full of coded trivia, movies within movies. Nothing as high toned as what Arthur Miller smuggled into *The Misfits* (1961), but then Mamie firing an elbow into the overamorous ribs of ex-hubby Ray Anthony wasn't intended for the uptown crowd. John Drew Barrymore dealt pot from the store in his glove compartment in *High School Confidential!* Tuesday Weld's bra strap broke in *Sex Kittens Go to College*, and Brigitte Bardot's younger sister, Mijanou, was on the same campus.

Who was that chasing Mamie up a tree at a beer bust? Why, it was Dick Contino, the famous draft dodging accordionist. And who cut a deliciously squirming Mamie free when she was tied to a bed at psychopathic Ray Danton's beach pad? You could tell by the sleepy eyes. Bob Mitchum's son, Jim. It all seemed funnier then. And yet people whose tastes have since reached the high plateau of subtitles fondly remember Mamie, dressed in jiggling sweater and tailored jeans, singing such deathless lines as, "You're as slimy as a salamander," and, "Come on, boys, and carry my bananas."

Realart's promotion of *Bride of the Gorilla* (1951) included special Halloween previews, one of which was my first experience at a midnight movie. The appearance of Barbara Payton on the screen was greeted with instant verbal approval, accompanied by whistling, stomping, and the ecstatic tribute of flying popcorn boxes, many of them sacrificed unemptied. It reminded me of a similar testimony rendered the previous year during Marilyn Monroe's brief scenes in *The Asphalt Jungle*. Marilyn, of course, went on to render her fragile talent to more exacting demands. But for Barbara Payton our popcorn enthusiasm was too late. She already was on the downward path, proof that the mostly mythical ethos of the Hollywood starlet occasionally touched living flesh.

In early publicity photos she bore a striking resemblance to Lana Turner. Once she parachuted into the back lot of a studio where tests were being held for the part of a stewardess. She was tired of running second to Tex Williams' horse in conventional Westerns for Universal-International. Her biggest brush with stardom was achieved by busting unannounced into a casting director's office at Cagney Productions. Fanning her legs with the retreating hem of her dress, she proclaimed, "Shit! It's a hot fucking day!" She got the part, James Cagney's girl friend in *Kiss Tomorrow Goodbye* (1950).

In late 1951 Tom Neal slugged Franchot Tone in a dispute over Barbara's mercurial affections. Hollywood was a nervous respecter of morality in the fifties. *Confidential* was soon to terrorize the industry to the delights of its millions of readers.

Real detectives, who lacked Philip Marlowe's finely tuned ethic, blew the whistle on every scandal in town. Only months before the Neal-Tone fracas, Fox and MGM were interested in her. Within a few years she had made her last Hollywood movie.

Around town they knew she made at least one more film. The stills were circulated in sealed unmarked envelopes, and studio doors closed to her forever. A producer she occasionally slept with was in the habit of leaving her three hundred

WARNERS
Kiss Tomorrow Goodbye: Prophetic film title for Barbara Payton, who went from leads opposite such as James Cagney to motel studios with rolled-down blinds and unscripted parts played entirely from memory (see insert).

dollars before he departed in the morning. Barbara looked in her purse one morning and found only a hundred. The producer explained, "Three hundred was a long time ago. To me, right now, you're worth about a hundred dollars."

She drifted around, down to Mexico where she put on weight, back north to stucco anonymity. She wrote poetry: "Love is a memory/Time cannot kill." In a few more years her price was down to forty dollars. Police photos of her arrest for prostitution revealed a plump blonde, eyes red from crying, her puffy face a reminder that the body treats alcohol as a fat. Nobody could believe she was the starlet who once looked like Lana Turner.

In the tit culture of the fifties women were always broads, the relation between aggressive sexuality and dehumanization as inevitable as a knee-jerk reflex. In a cover story on Marilyn Monroe a *Newsweek* writer remembered her as an "oversexed moll" in *The Asphalt Jungle*. Look again. Memories of Monroe have become inextricably linked with those of a legion of imitators who emphasized the tough girlie-mag image she projected only once.

MGM touted Elaine Stewart as a rival to Monroe, but by the end of the decade she was still bathing in rain barrels to attract attention. Peggie Castle caught a slug in the belly from Mike Hammer in *I, the Jury* (1953). You had the feeling she deserved a lot worse. Marla English, with a face as impassive as a totem pole, was AIP's *The She Creature* (1956). And Mari Blanchard, the toughest cookie of them all, was a *She Devil* (1957).

For anyone who missed the latent menace associated with fifties sexual fantasy, *Attack of the 50-Foot Woman* (1958) provided the ultimate poetic text. Voluptuous Allison Hayes grows so large that her papier-mâché foot occupies the entire corner of her bedroom. One night she goes looking for her wandering husband, dwarfing the landscape as she tramps across the midnight horizon in her nightgown. You can bet she scares all the men for miles around.

More recently, *Carnal Knowledge* (1971) has invited us to consider the long-range damage of the girlie mag mentality. Jack Nicholson explains to his old college chum, Art Garfunkel, that he almost got married but the girl lacked two inches on her tits and three on her hips—a precise view of femininity obviously culled from the collective wisdom of pinup captions.

12
Adapted for the Screen

The writers were ribbing Jerry Wald again. At the 1958 Screenwriters Annual Award Dinner Jack Carson, playing the energetic producer noted for his zealous appetite for literary properties, announced the latest haul. It included: *An Introduction to the Outline of Human Stupidity,* the story of RKO and Howard Hughes; two surly memos from David O. Selznick, $80,-000 the pair; *Roget's Thesaurus*; and for his first musical, *Arthritis and Common Sense.*

The sketch by John Michael Hayes caught the eccentric catholicism of Wald's taste, but missed the flavor of his frequently serious pronouncements about the problems of adaptation for the screen. Wald once polled forty-three hundred librarians to find out what he should buy for films. The "long-sellers" particularly attracted him, books which lasted beyond the hustle of a hard quick season. The librarians told the producer of *Peyton Place* that sex ranked last among the interests of readers, and that Willa Cather was among the most popular novelists of all time. Wald couldn't do much about the novels of Miss Cather. Her estate specifically stated that none of her books ever could be sold to the movies. But from what the librarians told him he purchased D.

H. Lawrence's *Sons and Lovers*, Budd Schulberg's *The Harder They Fall*, and William Faulkner's *The Sound and the Fury*.

Eventually, all three novels were made into movies. The least prestigious novel, Schulberg's boxing story, possibly turned out best as a film, although *Sons and Lovers* (1960) was widely admired and nominated for an Academy Award. There could be no doubt about the worst. Faulkner's novel emerged as a murky and static film creditably restrained from lapsing into Gothic soap opera. What, after all, could be expected from a novel which with brilliant audacity opens with the sustained stream-of-consciousness of a dumb idiot? How is that filmed? Faulkner must have wondered himself. Wald reported to the trade press, without an apparent trace of irony, that "Faulkner puts no restrictions on the production other than that he not be required to read the script or see the picture."

Others wondered why Wald wanted to film the book in the first place. The intricate interweaving of time and memory flux in the minds of three members of the Compson family was a high point in novelistic achievement. But what were the implications for film? In an article for *Films in Review*, Wald quoted approvingly screenwriter Philip Dunne on the obligations in adapting novels for the screen. The adaptation should ". . . express the intent of the novelist . . . capture the spirit and inner essence, the style of the original. . . ." Most importantly, the audience familiar with the book should say of the film, "That's exactly the way I remember it."

By these criteria, inexact as they are, *The Sound and the Fury* (1959) would have raised a ripple of recognition only in those familiar with the novel through a *Barron's* outline. In fact, it would be difficult to think of a work of fiction which more clearly demonstrates the intransigent differences between novel and film. Most theorists of the two media conclude that the invisible inward life of the mind—especially the interiorized sensibility rendered by stream-of-consciousness—resists translation into film imagery. Probably we will, never know what the forty-three hundred librarians told Jerry Wald to convince him to buy Faulkner's novel. But we can guess at some of the probable motives by recalling the mania for literary adaptation that dominated the fifties.

Smaller pictures with miniscule budgets had long existed on scripts dreamed up down the hall by contract writers. About a year before its disappearance into Allied Artists, Monogram proudly announced that it was stepping up its flow of originals. But that was just more Bowery Boys and Bomba of the Jungle. And where were those scripts supposed to come from? Ernest Hemingway?

Prestige pictures from major studies were a trickier matter. The tough Eastern banking money demanded every edge provided by cold analysis in securing the return of its investment. Stars and literary properties of proven appeal were a form of collateral frequently demanded. As the postwar pinch continued into the early fifties, a trend away from expensive acquisitions developed. In 1950 nearly seven out of ten pictures were produced from scripts written originally for the movies, thereby reducing one of the most costly factors in many films: the supposedly "pre-sold" literary property for which small fortunes were regularly paid. Although no movie written originally for the screen had won the Academy's Best Picture award since Leo McCarey's *Going My Way* (1944), Billy Wilder's *Sunset Boulevard* was nominated in 1950 and went on to box-office success.

Nonetheless the trend toward originals was short-lived. Joseph L. Mankiewicz' *No Way Out*, released almost simultaneously with *All About Eve*, was one of the most violently attacked pictures of the decade. The crazies flowering in soil fertilized by Joe McCarthy called it a commie nigger-lovers' film. Exhibitors, stung by a nationally reported attack on them attributed to Mankiewicz, begged for someone to send them a Bob Hope picture before their theaters closed. Billy Wilder fared no better. Paramount changed the name of *Ace in the Hole* to *The Big Carnival*, but it was a flop under either title. Wilder directed no more originals until the end of the decade. *The Well*, written by the inventive team of Russell Rouse and Clarence Greene, was, as one theater owner put it, as "popular as snow in the lobby."

In early 1952 *Film Daily* reporter Patti Alicoate wrote an article which observed, "Originals no longer prime source of screen material as 1950–51 trend is reversed." In the first quarter of the year studios and independents bought more than thirty novels compared to only nine originals, "no longer clinging to the theory that a story written solely for film production makes a better movie." In Hollywood "theory" tends to be the name given to the dyspeptic caterwauling heard from the front office when the numbers go bad. At the end of 1951 revenues had dropped for the fifth consecutive year since the end of the war.

For the remainder of the decade Hollywood embraced the "pre-sold" concept like a spurned lover trying to restore his charm with an open check book. It was the era of the big winner, the picture so fantastically successful its riches would pay the burial costs for the studio's disasters. Name writers, hit plays, pop novels were wooed cash-in-hand. When Irving Rapper began work on *The Glass Menagerie* (1950), a studio official told him he didn't see the project as "a great movie." More probably it would be "a prestige piece." On occasion Hollywood was willing to pay for the imported luxury of prestige, and in the fifties the highly sexed, poetically ambiguous plays of Tennessee Williams combined the new race for adult entertainment with the somewhat older sport of bounty hunting along the Great White Way.

If Williams' *The Glass Menagerie* was worth $150,000,

then *A Streetcar Named Desire* was worth more than twice as much. Modest novels of middling success regularly brought six figures. Richard Powell received $150,000 for *The Philadelphian*; Niven Busch more than that for the unfilmed *California Street*. A few weeks on *The New York Times* bestseller list doubled the value of a book. An appearance on the *Times* list raised the ante for John Farris' *Harrison High* from $60,000 to $100,000 plus a percentage of the gate. Broadway plays like *The Solid Gold Cadillac* and *Anastasia* brought between three and four hundred thousand each. For the supersmash *West Side Story* Seven Arts paid $350,000 and 10 percent of the world net. Michael Todd went to over a million for *Oklahoma!*.

Pierre Boulle's piddling five grand for *The Bridge Over the River Kwai* jumped to $150,000 and 5 percent of the gross for his next novel. The generosity of Warners made the front pages of the trades when the studio dealt out $1,500,000, most of it for three purchases: *The Dark at the Top of the Stairs*, a play by William Inge; *A Summer Place*, a novel by Sloan Wilson, whose earlier *The Man in the Gray Flannel Suit* was quintessential fifties schlock and as a movie the most expensively ballyhooed in Fox's history; and *Ice Palace,* a novel by Edna Ferber. Miss Ferber already had banked a million five as her cut of the take from *Giant*, at the time the highest return from a literary property in the history of Hollywood's patronage of the arts.

By 1958 less than half of the industry's movies were from original scripts. Contract writers, who had slipped from well over a hundred in the early fifties to around thirty by 1954, were now as rare around the studio commissary as the three-toed sloth. MGM announced it was preparing to film sixteen novels, the most prodigious transformation of fiction into film in the roaring lion's history.

Fox, complaining of an "acute shortage of pre-sold materials," decided to create its own. Grace Metalious was given

$265,000 to resurrect Peyton Place. Gossip columnist Sheilah Graham was nudged into commemorating for posterity her affair with F. Scott Fitzgerald. Bantam agreed to spend $100,000 promoting the paperback edition, with the assurance that Gregory Peck would be along shortly to impersonate Graham's *Beloved Infidel.*

Backed by New American Library and headed by public relations expert Ted Loeff, the Literary Projects Company carried the process of creating instant best sellers one step further. It arranged multiple tie-ins among producers and publishers to guarantee mutually profitable exploitation of novels sold to the movies prior to publication. In some cases, prior to their existence outside the hungry imaginations of their authors. Among Literary Projects' initial charges was an ex-screenwriter whose first novel, *The Sins of Philip Fleming,* was so execrable it was published by a subsidy house. But Ted Loeff thought they all might do very much better with Irving Wallace's next book, *The Chapman Report.*

Hollywood had entered the business of producing nonbooks for nonreaders. It was mind boggling. Some thought it wasn't even good business. Producer Lou Morheim attacked the "pre-sold" theory on the grounds that huge prices were paid for books which sold no more than thirty thousand copies in a country of 170 million. William Fadiman, a former executive story editor at both MGM and Columbia, said the creation of pseudo-books was proliferating the flow of inferior products unworthy of either the film or the novel.

Literary historian Albert Van Nostrand hardly could have agreed more. Surveying in 1960 what he called *The Denatured Novel,* Van Nostrand charged that "the movies have eroded the novel form more than anything else in the novel's history." In the fifties the allegation as easily could have been reversed. The Hollywood genuflection in the direction of the older literary culture often brought it not only to its

COLUMBIA

The Caine Mutiny: José Ferrer douses Fred MacMurray with drink demonstrating that intellectuals are all wet, key theme in Herman Wouk novels *Caine Mutiny* and *Marjorie Morningstar,* as well as in popular movies based on them. Arthur Franz is third man looking on.

knees but flat onto its face. The skittish audience had no reason to feel betrayed by such films as *Desiree* (1954), *The Silver Chalice* (1954), or *Another Time, Another Place* (1958). Even if, as in the case of *The Egyptian,* only a third of the novel was used, the pact was maintained of making the reader feel the best intentions of the book had been honored. If the crowds stayed home—as they frequently did —it was for some vaporish quirk as sociologically elusive as steam off a tea kettle, and not for fear of having their literary sensibilities offended.

Even that weightless piece of Lucite, *Marjorie Morningstar* (1958), was, if anything, faithful to Herman Wouk's continuing defense of middle-American virtue from the fleshly agnosticism of irresponsible bohem intellectuals. Just to show that no hard feelings toward Art were intended, Natalie Wood, in giving up the despicably unsuccessful Gene Kelly, earns in compensation the respectful attentions of another playwright, Martin Milner. Of course, as only we and Natalie's parents knew all along, Milner was the better catch. His plays are successful. As his backer, Jesse White, tells us, smiling around his stogie, "They have happy endings!"

With mediocre fiction, mutilation of the original wasn't a charge the adapting screenwriter lost much sleep over. But Jerry Wald's "long-seller" provoked deeper obligations to the craft of adaptation and the art of film writing. For an age in which Douglas Sirk's *Written on the Wind* (1956) and *The Tarnished Angels* (1957) "become more impressive with each passing year," it is hard to recall the frequent contempt in which movies were held less than twenty years ago.

In *How Not to Write a Play* drama critic Walter Kerr assumed without controversy that "an imagined contest between the finest film ever made and the finest play ever written must inevitably end in victory for the play." The reason? "Words are subtler than pictures." Novelist Margaret Kennedy wrote in *The Mechanized Muse* that, after all, screen writing "is no more a work of literature than is the recipe for a pudding." Hollywood was drawn to the "long-sellers" out of a curious mixture of cultural inferiority and the usual greedy hustle. Literary classics not only were "pre-sold," they were also investments in a process of osmosis by which plain old movies could be elevated to the level of cinema.

And so some of the great bombs of the fifties resulted from an effort to torment the secret of Art out of an older and supposedly superior medium. The more uniquely created the novel, the less likely the film makers would be to find cinematic equivalents for what were essentially literary qualities. Wald setting his screenwriters to work on Faulkner's *The Sound and the Fury* was like sending boys into the woods to chop down a redwood with knives.

Hemingway was equally hacked up on the way to the movies. With good reason he never liked the films made from his novels and stories. *The Snows of Kilimanjaro* (1952) he referred to contemptuously as The Snows of Zanuck. David O. Selznick's myopic plans for *A Farewell to Arms* (1957) resulted in the replacement of John Huston, who at least escaped with his honor. Screenwriter Peter Viertel told Mike Steen that Hollywood wanted only Hemingway's name. The wrong people bought the books and then destroyed them. Viertel was in a unique position to judge. He had written the screenplay for *The Sun Also Rises* (1957).

Viertel also wrote the screenplay for *The Old Man and the Sea* (1958), which he knew to be one of Hemingway's favorite books, the one that had restored his reputation after the embarrassment of *Across the River and into the Trees.* Hemingway especially hoped for a good movie out of *Old Man,* but it was not to be. Viertel's devotion to the literal prose of the novel amounted in the opening scenes, and periodically thereafter, to reading Hemingway to pictures. The introspective thoughts of the Old Man, when uttered aloud by Spencer Tracy, grew increasingly ludicrous. They ranged from conversations with the Big Fish, through a lecture on Man to a bird, before descending to the repeatedly unanswered query, "How do you feel, hand?" Even the symbolic fight with the Fish turned out poorly. Director John Sturges readily admitted that the film "was technically the sloppiest picture I ever made." Hemingway swore off films forever after *The Old Man and the Sea.*

Much worse, and, perhaps, the most disappointing literary adaptation of the decade, was Dore Schary's production *Lonelyhearts* (1958), based on the then recently rediscovered Nathanael West novel of the thirties. Schary's first independent film after being eased out at MGM was an unmitigated disaster. In a famous *Esquire* piece Dwight Macdonald reamed Hollywood for "converting *Miss Lonelyhearts* into *Stover at Yale,*" and in the process producing a film about as cinematic "as the proceedings of the American Iron & Steel Institute."

* * *

In amiable contrast to these stuttering translations from big time Art were a number of excellent films descended from distinctly minor novels. Stanley Kubrick, who with *Killer's Kiss* had already proved that, at the very least, he could make an interesting movie out of a New York street map, drafted a tense and imaginatively visualized thriller, *The Killing*, from Lionel White's *Clean Break*. Even better was *The Night of the Hunter* (1955), with Robert Mitchum as the malignantly mad Preacher. Charles Laughton, directing his only film, worked with cameraman Stanley Cortez from a script by the brilliant James Agee to construct a movie as structurally simple as a ballad and as atmospherically horrific as a child's nightmare. All of this from a rather inflated and hysterical novel.

So great was the mystique of the Novel, however, that Budd Schulberg couldn't resist tampering with the Oscar-winning *On the Waterfront* to turn his original screenplay

UNITED ARTISTS
The Night of the Hunter: Robert Mitchum terrorizes Billy Chapin in only film directed by Charles Laughton.

into a less satisfactory work of fiction. In the *Saturday Review*, Schulberg discussed his reversal of the usual transition from novel to film. Fiction offered the opportunity "to search the interior drama of the heart," while avoiding the tyranny of the ninety-minute movie. Unfortunately, the novelization of *Waterfront* sacrificed the virtuous pressure of economy necessary to film. The focus spread and shifted, losing intensity as it drifted from Terry Malloy's painful birth of conscience—so well realized by Brando in the film —to the less interesting and far less dramatic garrulous sermonizing of Father Barry.

Schulberg's *Saturday Review* essay captured well the contradictory affiliations of the novelist also committed to screen writing. The "novel is a wide-angle lens. Broader even than Cinerama. The real 3-D," Schulberg wrote. The struggling metaphor revealed the literary culture's barely concealed contempt for film. Novels, after all, were the real movies, "still the essential civilizing influence." Tensions between artisans in either medium weren't helped by such home-grown Hollywood theory as Niven Busch's public remark that "a bootblack at any studio . . . knows more about what makes a good story than an English major at an Ivy League college."

The rebuff was as good a reason as any for the English major to stay home and write his novel, keeping as much geographical distance as possible between himself and such Yahoo sentiments. Rather than corrupting the course of contemporary American fiction, the movies simply tended to ignore it. The most interesting work of the decade seldom reached the screen. Vance Bourjaily's novels never got a tumble, and where was Saul Bellow's *The Adventures of Augie March* or Herbert Gold's *The Man Who Was Not with It*? Near the end of the early fifties' cycle of black problem pictures Ralph Ellison's *Invisible Man* was published. To the movies the novel was as invisible as Ellison's black protagonist. If in 1955, instead of a short story called "Catch-18" in *New World Writing*, Joseph Heller's completed novel, *Catch-22*, had appeared, the impossibility of filming it would have been an assumption as reflexive as the contraction of the pupil under the stimulation of too much light.

For the serious American novelist of the fifties the movies represented a form of cultural oblivion to be resisted as long as the rigors of the breadline permitted. Edmund Wilson had warned them what happened to the Boys in the Back Room. Great writers of the recent past had gone to Hollywood to be misused and humiliated, and, worse, silenced as artists.

Everyone remembered Scott Fitzgerald pathetically trying to reclaim his fame in an industry the politics of which he never understood. The stories about Faulkner were legion. S. J. Perelman recalled a prowl car picking Faulkner up for the eccentric act of walking in Beverly Hills. The police thought he was casing the fancy homes for a gang of jewel thieves. And then there was the story about the lady screenwriter who turned him in to the studio biggies for drinking in his office. To novelist Shelby Foote, Faulkner confided, "Hollywood is the only place in the world where a man can get stabbed in the back while climbing a ladder."

Whatever the dire economic state of the young novelist at least he didn't face the indignity of a total blacklist in publishing. And what was the use of going to Hollywood anyway? "The screenplay is not an autonomous art form, and never has been," wrote Charles Van Nostrand. All they wanted out there was "some new twist of some old and salable ideas. . . . But the film cannot accommodate the novel's complexity."

J. D. Salinger heroically hid *The Catcher in the Rye* from the camera, despite offers which obviously would have made his life as a recluse easier. But he had sold his story "Uncle Wiggily in Connecticut" to RKO, where it was turned into a wet hankie called *My Foolish Heart* (1950). When *Paris Review* asked Nelson Algren how long he worked on the script of *The Man With the Golden Arm*, he quickly summarized his career on the coast. "I went out there for a thousand a week, and I worked Monday, and I got fired Wednesday. The guy that hired me was out of town Tuesday." Earlier Algren had informed the readers of *The Nation* that he had sold his novel to the movies in order to buy a house in Indiana. Norman Mailer denied a report in Archer Winsten's column in the *New York Post* that he had thrown mashed potatoes at producer Paul Gregory. In *Advertisements For Myself* he publicly disassociated himself from the movie of *The Naked and the Dead* ultimately produced by Gregory. Mailer claimed that his only sin was to sell the novel to Hollywood "after years of protecting its chastity."

The Naked and the Dead was the sort of bad adaptation that prompted images of violation to spring up in the minds of both critics and filmgoers familiar with the book. Even the screenwriters, Denis and Terry Sanders, tried to shake loose from responsibility for the picture. The centering event of Mailer's novel was the collision of wills between the burned-out radical, Lt. Hearn, and the neo-fascist, General Cummings. In the movie Hearn's important political past, inflammable by Hollywood standards, was reduced to a flashback of Cliff Robertson cavorting with what looked like the chorus line of a recently shelved musical. Some politics.

Still, not all novelists could complain that their best work was mugged by barbarians on the way to the screen. Daniel Taradash's adaptation of *From Here to Eternity* was less embarrassing to James Jones than his own subsequent novels. Theodore Dreiser's awkward fiction often hit the nail on the head only after smashing everyone on the thumb in the process. As *A Place in the Sun* (1951), *An American Tragedy* was well treated by George Stevens and an excellent cast headed by Montgomery Clift. Of William Wyler's *Carrie*

Marty: From left, Walter Kelley, Robin Morse, and Ernest Borgnine study girlie magazines symbolizing Saturday night fantasies of aging bachelors.

(1952) at least it could be said that the intentions were honorable. After working with Wyler on the filming of her novel *The Friendly Persuasion,* Jessamyn West told him she thought "movie making might be for the twentieth century what cathedral building was for the Middle Ages." Just the same, she was glad when he decided not to cast Jane Russell as Eliza.

Hollywood's most ironic inheritance from another medium occurred in the mid-fifties. In early 1956, *Daily Variety* noted with evident amusement that "the studios now are even dipping into TV to find feature material." And no wonder. The Motion Picture Academy had just bypassed three expensive Broadway adaptations—*Mister Roberts, Picnic,* and *The Rose Tattoo*—to honor as Best Picture of 1955 a black-and-white sleeper about an unmarried butcher and a remaindered girl who was not such a dog after all. *Marty* (1955) violated every tenet of the conventional wisdom of the CinemaScope Era. Rod Steiger, the TV Marty in the original telecast on the Goodyear Playhouse in 1953, was already engaged, and so the role went to Fatso of *From Here to Eternity*, Ernest Borgnine. Betsy Blair was the schoolteacher he meets at the neighborhood dance. Neither was a star. Author Paddy Chayefsky described the five-hundred-thousand-dollar budget as mostly "buttons and bones." But director Delbert Mann, like Chayefsky, was from television, where budgets were even lower. The subject matter, a sort of American *I Vitelloni* (1953), was low key, intimate, and about as glamorous as the garbage cans Borgnine kicked to celebrate his break with the Saturday-night-boys'-gang mentality of his aging bachelor friends.

As angry novelists like Nelson Algren vacated the Garden of Allah to return to their real work, the discontented survivors of television's golden days of Studio One, Kraft Television Theater, and Playhouse 90 met them coming the other way. The serious novelist was used to a purity of intention seldom possible in film projects where the budget ran to several hundred times what a publisher occasionally risked on a difficult piece of fiction. Live television drama disappeared as production costs rose, and sponsors became increasingly obsessed with ratings as an expression of advertising costs per thousand viewers. To the TV playwright the movies offered the frustrating but familiar problem of cooperative enterprise together with a freedom of expression no longer possible in commercial television of the later fifties.

Late in 1958, Paddy Chayefsky told David Susskind on "Open End" how it was on television in the good old days, the good old days being only four years earlier. You went to a producer like Fred Coe and told him you had an idea. "What is it?" Coe would ask. "I want to write a love story about a fat butcher in the Bronx," Chayefsky would say. "And what else?" "That's all." Coe would give it a minute to simmer and say, "Go ahead, write it." "You'll do it?"

UNITED ARTISTS
Patterns: Everett Sloane, second from left, and Van Heflin, foreground right, watch Ed Begley die of seizure in the hallway in best of movies based on Rod Serling's television plays of the fifties.

"We'll do it." And it was a deal. Now things were different. The excitement was gone, and television, like radio before it, was becoming an anonymous diversion designed to sell equally anonymous soap to Mencken's same old booboisie.

Conversely, the movies, in their desperate days, were opening new areas of subject matter. The plays television prohibited could be filmed. Chayefsky followed the spectacular success of *Marty* with adaptations of two of his other television plays, *The Catered Affair* (1956) and *The Bachelor Party* (1957). Next he wrote an original, *The Goddess* (1958), loosely based on the life of Marilyn Monroe, and then scripted *Middle of the Night* (1959) from his own Broadway play. Other adaptations from television included Reginald Rose's *Crime in the Streets* (1956) and *Twelve Angry Men* (1957); Rod Serling's *Patterns* and *The Rack*; J. P. Miller's *The Rabbit Trap* (1959); and Gore Vidal's *Visit to a Small Planet* (1960).

In their pinched, constricted visual design and talky

thematic seriousness, many of these movies wore rather conspicuously their origins as liberal television plays. However, in the popular cycle of business films, *Patterns* was one of the few in which matters of conscience held the screen longer than it takes to drink a martini and order a plug-in phone at 21. And *Twelve Angry Men* was a tour de force in which not the crime but the jury system was the center of attention.

In a 1957 letter to Murray Kempton reprinted in *Additional Dialogue,* screenwriter Dalton Trumbo observed, "Hollywood is as necessary to the intellectuals as the nigrah to his cracker neighbors. We're going down, boys, but look at *him*." For the novelist the movies were slumming, at best a way to pick up change until the writer returned to his more honorable craft. Television playwrights, by contrast, escaped upward to a medium even less despised than the one from which late in the decade they felt driven. The most prolific of them, Paddy Chayefsky, learned to live with low budgets, independent productions, and distribution problems. Musing on the tough fate of his darkest film, *The Goddess,* Chayefsky noted philosophically that, after all, "you cannot put a picture starring Kim Stanley and Lloyd Bridges into the Radio City Music Hall at Easter." The fact that you could put it anywhere was in some ways a measure of the changes occurring in the film markets of the fifties.

Only the next year the Music Hall intrepidly played *The Journey*, a movie about the abortive Hungarian Revolution of 1956 in which Yul Brynner portrayed the first sympathetic Communist seen in an American dramatic film in over a decade. The cultural surprise was mitigated by a particularly patriotic Rockettes stage show.

13
Into
the Movie
Age

The American generation born since 1930 cannot read. . . . With only token recourse to the printed word, for more than a decade the radio, the talking movie, the picture-magazine and the comic-book have served all the cultural and recreational needs of the generation of adults now upon us. For them, the printed word is on its way out.

GERSHON LEGMAN: *Love & Death* (1949)

My friends are still recovering from the thirteen-year-old baby sitter who corrected us all on some minor points in the film career of Carole Lombard. She was right, of course. And there was no picture book filmography for her to lean on. She learned it all, and much more, from watching old movies on television.

From the time they are wee tots teen-agers are said to spend about twenty hours a week in front of the tube. As high school graduates, they have logged something over fifteen thousand hours of television viewing, compared to less than eleven thousand hours of schooling in the same period. Media experts estimate that before college a teen-ager has seen some five hundred feature films on television. In the case of film buffs the figure easily could be four to five times that number.

Going off to college, the student for whom film has become the dominant cultural interest has a choice of over six hundred schools offering nearly six thousand courses in film and television. In almost two hundred schools he can major in film, and in more than fifty he can receive a degree, often including a doctorate. According to George Stevens Jr., the director of the American Film Institute, "Academic interest in all the moving-image technology has grown with such rapidity in the last few years that now nearly one-third of all U.S. four-year colleges offer courses in film and television."

I don't know what comparable educational possibilities existed in the fifties, but despite a university education received entirely in California, I met only one person who majored in film. He was the son of a distinguished director and wanted to make pictures himself, not write about them. Currently, well over twenty thousand people are studying film or television. Of those studying film about as many want to write about them as want to make them. The implications are clear. We are well along toward institutionalizing our responses to film and creating an elite body of consumers capable of discussing jump cuts and freeze frames with the authority of a film editor on a busman's holiday. Harold Ross once told screenwriter Nunnally Johnson that reviewing movies was for "women and fairies." Soon it will be mostly for university-trained historians brandishing doctorates on the Dark Imagination of Edgar Ulmer.

In the fifties the cultural atmosphere was quite different. Kingsley Amis wrote an Art Films column for *Esquire*; *Time* reviewed movies under the heading Cinema. But for most of the young people I knew films were usually flicks, an affectionate term suggesting pleasantly fugitive experience outside the claustrophobic bounds of high culture. The same films we regarded as amusingly expendable are treated these days to the sort of careful scrutiny we reserved for the Great American Novel.

The novels that emerged at the end of World War II were

among the last to address themselves to a widely shared national experience. Thereafter the most critically admired examples of the form became increasingly convoluted and stingy. We liked them that way. Criticism had taught us to attend to technical facility and architectural structure. As a student at Berkeley, I remember sitting in all-night donut shops conducting precious conversations about the metaphorical ambiguity of William Golding. We called novels "artifacts," a term that exposed both our love of jargon and the dusty archeological posturing of our expeditions across the grim deserts of modern fiction. Malcolm Cowley traveled the campuses to find student writers who had not the slightest narrative impulse. Nonetheless, they were deeply worried that in their manuscripts they had mismanaged the judicious arrangement of symbols. What bores we all were.

What was wrong was that we were too tightly packed with high culture, too bombarded with institutional demands to respond to still more books in increasingly bookish ways. We needed out; we needed air. And so we went to the movies, the flicks, using them as the speediest available antidote to the toxic effects of uninterrupted higher education. However trashy, however corny, the movies provided a ready sense of community, a shared mythology no more arcane than bone-deep memories on which we had grown up. These qualities could be especially refreshing if you were coming off a three-hour seminar in which you had survived papers on the sperm imagery in *Moby Dick* and the theme of the *isolato* in the poetry of Edwin Arlington Robinson.

Most important, in the fifties no official response was required of us at the movies. Critical hype and academic stratification were either nonexistent or in low profile. We had to respond for ourselves, to judge for ourselves. Nobody was at our shoulder waiting to add up the test scores. There was no competition and no prize. There were few authorities and none whose utterances were regularly published in book

form. As George Bluestone noted in 1957, "So far, no
American writer has attempted a full theoretical analysis of
our most influential cultural milieu."

The critical apparatus that surrounded the literary scene
had yet to be erected into parallel scaffolding around the
motion picture medium. James Agee no longer wrote reviews.
Robert Warshow was dead. The standard histories of the
earlier years of film such as Terry Ramsaye's *A Million And
One Nights*, Benjamin B. Hampton's *A History of the Movies*,

UNITED ARTISTS
Beat the Devil: "The bold adventure
that beats them all" turned out to be a
put-on of the caper genre which puzzled
audiences still expecting straight Bogey
from the forties.

and Lewis Jacobs' *The Rise of the American Film* were all long out of print. For that matter, so were Parker Tyler's more recent *The Hollywood Hallucination* and *Magic and Myth of the Movies*. For a good part of the decade *Esquire* lived without a movie critic. At the Los Angeles *Times* the chief reviewer liked anything with pageantry and everything from MGM.

I discovered *Beat the Devil, Killer's Kiss,* and *Invasion of the Body Snatchers* (1956) on my own, and only much later learned that they were objects of cult admiration. For the city hip of the seventies such cultural innocence is long past. On good authority I've been told that since 1960 more books on film have been published than all the titles printed in the preceding half century. While I haven't taken a body count, I don't doubt it. Only the other day I was reading a major work by a greatly admired young film critic. Of Kubrick's *2001: A Space Odyssey* (1968), he wrote, "The elegant simplicity of its architectural trajectories is the harmonic opposite of its galactic polymorphism." The book has been described as a landmark in film criticism, and this I wouldn't doubt either, although I regret it. It gives me a bad case of *déjà vu*. Happily, the movies, for the very reasons they have often been despised—their origin in collective commercial enterprise—are less susceptible than the novel to the deadly embrace of pretentious criticism.

For myself, I look forward to the widely promised golden flowering of the movie age. So does my friend Ed. In the fifties Ed was going to be a novelist. Today, he sells real estate, but as we sit in this restaurant, his son tells us about the movie his fifth-grade class is making. The boy's screenplay, a mystery story, is being filmed in "80 mm.," a modest misconception which we gently reduce to the more probable 16 mm. The movie is part of a national contest won the previous year by a competing school with a documentary on the Daughters of the American Revolution. The D.A.R. liked the film so much it purchased a print for its archives. "They won't like this one though," says the boy. "Everybody gets shot." And Ed smiles with paternal pride, while trying to teach the kid how to use a knife and fork in conjunction when cutting tough meat.

Selected Bibliography

ALGREN, NELSON, "Hollywood Djinn," *The Nation*, 177 (July 25, 1953), 68–70.

ALLOWAY, LAWRENCE, *Violent America: the Movies, 1946–1964*. New York, 1971.

ALBERT, HOLLIS, *The Dreams and the Dreamers*. New York, 1962.

———, "Movies Are Better Than the Stage," *Saturday Review*, 38 (July 23, 1955), 5–6, 31–32.

———, "Sexual Behavior in the American Movie," *Saturday Review*, 39 (June 23, 1956), 9–10, 38–40.

ANDERSON, JACK, and RONALD W. MAY, *McCarthy*. Boston, 1952.

ARDREY, ROBERT, "What Happened to Hollywood?," *The Reporter*, 16 (January 24, 1957), 19–22.

ASTRACHAN, SAM, "The New Lost Generation," *The New Republic*, 136 (February 4, 1957), 17–18.

BAKER, CARLOS, *Ernest Hemingway: A Life Story*. New York, 1969.

BARBOUR, ALAN G., *Days of Thrills and Adventure*. New York, 1970.

BAST, WILLIAM, *James Dean*. New York, 1956.

BAXTER, JOHN, *Science Fiction in the Cinema*. New York, 1970.

BAZIN, ANDRÉ, *What Is Cinema?* Vol. II. Berkeley and Los Angeles, 1971.

BEAN, ROBIN, and DAVID AUSTEN, "USA: Confidential," *Films and Filming*, 15 (November, 1968), 16–31.

BENEDICT, JOHN, "Movies Are Redder Than Ever," *American Mercury*, 41 (August, 1960), 3–23.

BESSIE, ALVAH, *Inquisition in Eden*. New York, 1965.

BIBERMAN, HERBERT, *Salt of the Earth*. Boston, 1965.

BLOOM, MURRAY TEIGH, "What Two Lawyers are doing to Hollywood," *Harper's Magazine*, 216 (February, 1958), 42–48.

BLUESTONE, GEORGE, "In Defense of 3-D," *Sewanee Review*, 64 (Fall, 1956), 683–689.

———, *Novels into Film*. Baltimore, 1957.

BRUSTEIN, ROBERT, "Reflections on Horror Movies," *Partisan Review*, 25 (Spring, 1958), 288–296.

CAREY, GARY, "The Many Voices of Donald Ogden Stewart," *Film Comment*, 6 (Winter, 1970–71), 74–79.

CARPOZI, GEORGE, *The Brigitte Bardot Story*. New York, 1961.

CERAM, C. W., *Archaeology of the Cinema*. New York, 1965.

CHAYEFSKY, PADDY, "Art Films—They're Dedicated Insanity," *Films and Filming*, 4 (May, 1958), 7, 32.

CLARENS, CARLOS, *An Illustrated History of the Horror Film*. New York, 1968.

COGLEY, JOHN, *Report on Blacklisting*. Vol. I: Movies. New York, 1956.

COHN, ROY, *McCarthy*. New York, 1968.

CONANT, MICHAEL, *Antitrust in the Motion Picture Industry*. Berkeley and Los Angeles, 1960.

COWLEY, MALCOLM, ed., *Writers at Work*. New York, 1959.

CUTTS, JOHN, "Bye Bye Musicals," *Films and Filming*, 10 (November, 1963), 42–45.

EBERT, ROGER, "Russ Meyer: King of the Nudies," *Film Comment*, 9 (January–February, 1973), 34–45.

FIEDLER, LESLIE, *An End to Innocence*. Boston, 1955.

Film Culture, Nos. 50–51 (Fall and Winter, 1970), special blacklist issue.

GEHMAN, RICHARD, "Confidential File On *Confidential*," *Esquire*, 46 (November, 1956), 67, 139–146.

GELMIS, JOSEPH, *The Film Director as Superstar*. New York, 1970.

GERBER, ALBERT B., *Bashful Billionaire*. New York, 1967.

GILLET, CHARLES, *The Sound of the City*. New York, 1970.

GOLDBERG, JOE, *Big Bunny*. New York, 1967.

GUILES, FRED LAWRENCE, *Norma Jean*. New York, 1969.

GUSSOW, MEL, *Don't Say Yes Until I Finish Talking*. New York, 1971.

HANO, ARNOLD, "The Sagging World of Jayne Mansfield," *Hollywood Uncensored*, Phil Hirsch, ed. New York, 1965.

HIGHAM, CHARLES, *Hollywood at Sunset*. New York, 1972.

———, *Hollywood Cameramen*. Bloomington, Ind., 1970.

HITCHENS, GORDON, "The Truth, The Whole Truth, and Nothing But The Truth About Exploitation Films," *Film Comment*, 2, No. 2 (1964), 1–13.

HOFSTADTER, RICHARD, *Anti-intellectualism in American Life*. New York, 1963.

————, *The Paranoid Style in American Politics.* New York, 1965.

HOLMES, JOHN CLELLON, *Nothing More to Declare.* New York, 1967.

HOUSEMAN, JOHN, "Hollywood Faces the Fifties," *Harper's Magazine,* 200 (April, 1950), 50–59 and (May, 1950), 51–59.

HRUSA, BERNARD, "On the Musical," *Film,* Nos. 14 and 15 (November–December, 1957), 16–19 and (January–February, 1958), 16–18.

JARVIE, I. C., *Movies and Society.* New York, 1970.

JENSEN, PAUL, "Paranoia in Hollywood," *Film Comment,* 7 (Winter, 1971–72), 36–45.

JOHNSON, WILLIAM, ed., *Focus On: The Science Fiction Film.* Englewood Cliffs, N. J., 1972.

KANTOR, BERNARD R., IRWIN R. BLACKER, and ANNE KRAMER, *Directors At Work.* New York, 1970.

KEMPTON, MURRAY, *Part of Our Time.* New York, 1955.

KITSES, JIM, "The Rise and Fall of the American West," *Film Comment,* 6 (Winter, 1970–71), 14–21.

KLEIN, ALEXANDER, "The Challenge of Mass Media," *Yale Review,* 39 (June, 1950), 675–691.

KNIGHT, ARTHUR, "Cheez it, the Cops!," *Saturday Review,* 37 (October 2, 1954), 43–44.

KNIGHT, ARTHUR, and HOLLIS ALPERT, "The History of Sex in Cinema: Part XVI, The Nudies," *Playboy,* 14 (June, 1967), 124–136, 177–188.

KOBAL, JOHN, *Gotta Sing Gotta Dance.* New York, 1970.

LARDNER, RING, JR., "My Life on the Blacklist," *The Saturday Evening Post,* 234 (October 14, 1961), 38–44.

LARKINS, ROBERT, "Hollywood and the Indian," *Focus on Film* (March–April, 1970), 44–53.

LEHMAN, MILTON, "Who Censors Our Movies?," *Look,* 18 (April 6, 1954), 86–92.

LIMBACHER, JAMES, "Widescreen Chronology," *Films in Review,* 6 (October, 1955), 403–405.

LINCOLN, FREEMAN, "The Comeback of the Movies," *Fortune,* 51 (February, 1955), 127–134, 155–158.

MACDONALD, DWIGHT, "No Art and No Box Office," *Esquire,* 51 (March, 1959), 62–66.

MC DONALD, GERALD D., "Origin of the Star System," *Films in Review,* 4 (November, 1953), 449–459.

MACGOWAN, KENNETH, *Behind the Screen.* New York, 1965.

MC VAY, DOUGLAS, *The Musical Film.* New York, 1967.

MALTIN, LEONARD, *Behind the Camera.* New York, 1971.

————, *Movie Comedy Teams.* New York, 1970.

MANKIEWICZ, JOSEPH L., "All About the Women in 'All About Eve,'" *New York,* 5 (October 16, 1972), 37–42.

MAPP, EDWARD, *Blacks in American Films.* Metuchen, N.J., 1972.

MAYER, ARTHUR L., "Are Movies 'Better Than Ever'?," *Saturday Review of Literature,* 33 (June 17, 1950), 9–10, 34–38.

————, "Myths and Movies," *Harper's Magazine,* 202 (June, 1951), 71–77.

MAYER, MARTIN, "The Apotheosis of James Dean," *Esquire,* 46 (December, 1956), 166, 242–246.

MILLER, MERLE, *The Judges and the Judged.* New York, 1952.

MILNE, TOM, *Losey on Losey.* New York, 1968.

MILNER, MICHAEL, *Sex on Celluloid.* New York, 1964.

MITGANG, HERBERT, "The Strange James Dean Death Cult," *Coronet,* 41 (November, 1956), 110–115.

MORIN, EDGAR, *The Stars.* New York, 1961.

"Movies: End of an Era?," *Fortune,* 39 (April, 1949), 99–102, 135–150.

NOBLE, PETER, *The Negro in Films.* London, 1948.

NURMI, MAILA, "The Ghost of James Dean," *Borderline,* 1 (January, 1964), 19–23.

PAYTON, BARBARA, *I Am Not Ashamed.* Los Angeles, 1963.

POPKIN, HENRY, "Liberal Unpolitics On Stage and Screen," *Commentary,* 23 (February, 1957), 161–166.

POSTER, WILLIAM, "Movies: The Death of the Hero," *American Mercury,* 72 (February, 1951), 225–229.

————, "Movies: Hollywood Caterers to the Middle Class," *American Mercury,* 73 (August, 1951), 82–91.

POTTER, CHARLES E., *Days of Shame.* New York, 1965.

PRATLEY, GERALD, *The Cinema of Otto Preminger.* New York, 1971.

RANDALL, RICHARD S., *Censorship of the Movies.* Madison, Wis., 1968.

"RKO: It's Only Money," *Fortune,* 47 (May, 1953), 122–127, 206–215.

SARRIS, ANDREW, *The American Cinema.* New York, 1968.

————, *Interviews With Film Directors.* New York, 1967.

SCHRADER, PAUL, "Notes on Film Noir," *Film Comment,* 8 (Spring, 1972), 8–13.

SCHULBERG, BUDD, "The Frightened City," *Nation's Business*, 37 (August, 1949), 36–38, 72.

——, "Why Write It When You Can't Sell It to the Movies?," *Saturday Review*, 38 (September 3, 1955), 5–6, 27.

SCHUMACH, MURRAY, *The Face On The Cutting Room Floor*. New York, 1964.

SCULLIN, GEORGE, "James Dean: The Legend and the Facts," *Look*, 20 (October 16, 1956), 120–128.

SEATON, GEORGE, "A Comparison of the Playwright and the Screen Writer," *Quarterly of Film, Radio, and Television*, 10 (September, 1956), 217–226.

SELDES, GILBERT, "Are the Foreign Films Better?," *Atlantic Monthly*, 184 (September, 1949), 49–52.

SHAFFER, HELEN B., "Changing Fortunes of the Movie Business," *Editorial Research Reports* (September 3, 1953), 609–626.

——, "Movie–Tv Competition," *Editorial Research Reports* (January 18, 1957), 43–61.

SILVER, ALAIN, "Mr. Film Noir Stays at the Table," *Film Comment*, 8 (Spring, 1972), 14–23.

STEDMAN, RAYMOND WILLIAM, *The Serials*. Norman, Okla., 1971.

STEEN, MIKE, *A Look At Tennessee Williams*. New York, 1969.

STONE, I. F., *The Haunted Fifties*. New York, 1963.

THOMAS, BOB, *King Cohn*. New York, 1967.

THOMPSON, HUNTER S., *Hell's Angels*. New York, 1967.

TRUMBO, DALTON, *Additional Dialogue*. New York, 1970.

VAN NOSTRAND, ALBERT, *The Denatured Novel*. New York, 1960.

VAUGHN, ROBERT, *Only Victims*. New York, 1972.

VIZZARD, JACK, *See No Evil*. New York, 1970.

WAGNER, GEOFFREY, *Parade of Pleasure*. New York, 1955.

WALD, JERRY, "Faulkner & Hollywood," *Films in Review*, 10 (March, 1959), 129–134.

——, "Screen Adaptation," *Films in Review*, 5 (February, 1954), 62–67.

WANGER, WALTER, and JOE HYAMS, *My Life With Cleopatra*. New York, 1963.

WARNER, JACK, *My First Hundred Years in Hollywood*. New York, 1965.

WARSHOW, ROBERT, *The Immediate Experience*. New York, 1962.

WEALES, GERALD, "Crazy, Mixed-up Kids Take Over," *The Reporter*, 15 (December 13, 1956), 40–41.

WEINBERG, MEYER, *TV in America*. New York, 1962.

WECHSLER, JAMES, *Reflections of an Angry Middle-Aged Editor*. New York, 1960.

WEST, JESSAMYN, *To See the Dream*. New York, 1957.

"What's Wrong With Television Drama," *Film Culture*, No. 19 (1959), 18–37.

WHITMAN, HOWARD, *The Sex Age*. New York, 1962.

WOLF, MARK, "Stop Frame: The History and Technique of Fantasy Film Animation," *Cinefantastique*, 1 (Winter, 1971), 6–21 and 2 (Spring, 1972), 8–17.

WOLFENSTEIN, MARTHA, and NATHAN LEITES, "The Good-Bad Girl," *Mass Culture: The Popular Arts in America*, Bernard Rosenberg and David Manning White, eds. New York, 1957.

Writers at Work (second series). New York, 1965.

ZINSSER, WILLIAM K., "The Bold and Risky World of 'Adult' Movies," *Life*, 48 (February 29, 1960), 78–86.

Index